A PARADISE
CALLED TEXAS

A PARADISE
CALLED TEXAS

by

Janice Jordan Shefelman

Illustrations by

Tom · Karl · Dan
Shefelman

EAKIN PRESS ⟨ᴇᴘ⟩ Fort Worth, Texas

Library of Congress Cataloging in Publication Data

Shefelman, Janice Jordan, 1930 —
   A Paradise Called Texas.

   Summary: Searching for a better life, Mina and her parents leave
their German fatherland in 1845 and sail to Texas where they find
hardship, tragedy, and adventure.
   [1. Texas — Fiction. 2. Emigration and immigration — Fiction]
I. Shefelman, Tom, ill. II. Shefelman, Karl, ill. III. Shefelman, Dan,
ill. IV. Title.
PZ7.S54115Par 1983   [Fic]   83-1754

STORIES FOR YOUNG AMERICANS SERIES

Published in the United States of America
By Eakin Press
An Imprint of Wild Horse Media Group
P.O. Box 331779
Fort Worth, Texas 76163
www.EakinPress.com

ISBN 0-89015-506-2

For Daddy

AUTHOR'S NOTE

A Paradise Called Texas is based on my German ancestors' immigration to Texas. Mina came with her mother and father and many other Germans when Texas was still a frontier. They were looking for a better life. Instead, they found hardship, tragedy, and adventure.

Mina is actually a combination of two girls. The first Mina died during an epidemic in New Braunfels some six months after arriving in Texas. Her father, my great-grandfather, named his second daughter Mina to ease his grief. I think he would be happy that his beloved *kleine* Mina lives on in my story.

As I came to know Mina better while writing her story, she talked me into letting her have more adventures. Some of them really did happen, and all of them *could* have happened. There was indeed a Chief Custaleta, a Lipan Apache, living in the hill country, but their meeting was Mina's idea.

CONTENTS

1

A STRANGER IN THE VILLAGE

Wehrstedt, Germany
May, 1845

School was dismissed at noon, and Mina ran home as fast as she could, along the winding village street. She did not wait for her cousins, because she had to tell Papa about the stranger.

"Papa, Papa!" Mina burst through the door into the big room. "There is a stranger in the village!"

Everyone in the room stopped still as Mina came in. Papa, Uncle Christian, and Opa were sitting at the oaken table in the center of the room. Mama and Aunt Sophie were bringing steaming bowls. Mina stood there looking at them, breathless from her run, her heart pounding within her chest.

"Now, Mina, come and sit here." Papa patted a place on the bench next to him.

Mina sat lightly beside him, and looked into his

broad face that was neatly framed with a fringe beard. Papa's sad eyes always calmed her.

"Now, tell me, Mina, about this stranger."

"Well, he came on a horse, and put up a notice on the schoolhouse about going to Texas to live. It says there is to be a new Germany in Texas — a paradise!" Mina could sit no longer. She jumped up, flicking her right braid over her shoulder. Facing Papa, she continued, "He is going to tell about Texas this very afternoon. Let us go and hear him . . . please, Papa."

"*Ja*, Ernst, you should go with the child." Opa leaned back in his chair at the head of the table. His deep-set eyes seemed to sparkle from under the thick eyebrows as he turned to look at Mina. She knew he was smiling even though his mouth was hidden in his grizzled beard and mustache.

"But there is much work to do in the field this afternoon," Papa said to his father.

"Well, Christian and I can work alone for today," Opa answered.

Uncle Christian looked sullen as always. Mama and Aunt Sophie had sat down at last when the other children came in — Christine and Hans. Christine smiled sweetly. Sometimes Mina wished she could be as serene and beautiful as Christine. But it was not possible. Feelings came bubbling up inside her, and she could not deny them. Mama always told her she must act more like a lady.

"Do you not have school this afternoon, Mina?" Mama asked.

"No, *Herr* Bremer has let out school for the rest of the day so that we can learn about Texas."

Papa laughed. "Very well, my *kleine* Mina, we shall go."

2

Papa had called her *kleine* Mina ever since she could remember. Her real name was Johanne Ernestine Wilhelmine Jordan, but she was called Mina for short.

The two families sat down to dinner. Mina bowed her head and listened as Opa said the grace in his deep resounding voice, filling the room up into the dark rafters.

Come, Lord Jesus, be our guest,
And let the food You gave be blessed.

Mina loved Opa's big house. It had been built years ago by his father. But someday Opa would give the farmstead to his first-born son, Christian. Then where would they go?

One thing was certain. They could not continue to live in this house. Papa and Uncle Christian had disagreements and were not fond of each other. No, without Opa here, it could not be their home.

Mina stood with Papa and Mama in the crowd of villagers gathered around the front door of the schoolhouse, waiting for the stranger to begin.

"Farmer folk of Wehrstedt . . . I come here to tell you of a wonderful opportunity, a chance to start a new life, farming your own land in that paradise of North America called Texas."

The stranger moved up to the top step and stood in front of the schoolhouse door. "My name is Johann Schneider, and I have been sent to your village by the *Adelsverein*, a group of noblemen who have purchased land in Texas for the benefit of German peasants."

He unrolled a map of North America, and asked a bystander to hold one side. "Now, here we have the Republic of Texas, a vast land — rich and fertile — just

3

waiting for German farmers to plant their seeds and reap their harvest."

Herr Schneider rolled up the map and continued. "Here in Germany there is little land left, and there are more and more people. But in Texas there is no limit to the land. Each family that signs a contract with the *Adelsverein* will receive three hundred and twenty acres of rich farmland."

There were sounds of astonishment from the crowd. "Three hundred and twenty acres! That is more than our whole village and farmlands put together."

Someone in the crowd held up his hand. "How much does it cost?"

"A good question," another said.

"Well, my friends, that is the best part of all," *Herr* Schneider answered. "For only six hundred gulden the *Adelsverein* will provide the land and transportation to Texas on a fine sailing ship. At the Texas port, wagons will be waiting to take you to the new colony where houses and schools will be built. And the *Adelsverein* also promises to provide food and supplies until a first harvest can be made." *Herr* Schneider held out his arms to the crowd. "All this for a mere six hundred gulden."

People began talking among themselves, but *Herr* Schneider continued. "Do not think that you would be leaving all friends and neighbors behind, for many families from villages only a few kilometers away have signed contracts to go — the Kaufmanns from Armstedt, the Engels from Westfeld. It will be like a new Germany in Texas."

Herr Schneider put on his hat. "I will return in a week with contracts for any to sign who may decide to go. The brig *Margaretha* will depart Bremerhaven at the end of the summer, so there is plenty of time for prepara-

4

tions." He stepped down and made his way to his horse.

All that land, thought Mina. Why, one would be as wealthy as a nobleman. Mina longed to see the world outside their little village. She had only been to Bad Salzdetfurth — two kilometers away — where rich people came to take the cure. But she longed to see great cities, the boundless ocean, and most of all America.

As they started walking home, Mina skipped. She felt excitement coursing through her body.

Papa turned to Mama. "Perhaps we should think about going to Texas, Minchen. It sounds very good." He looked at her, waiting.

"But Ernst, we cannot leave Wehrstedt. It is our home. Germany is our Fatherland." Mama smoothed back her blond hair that was coiled in a braid on the back of her head. "I could not leave our home to go to a wilderness."

"Minchen, we will never have a home and farm of our own here. And even my days as a linen weaver are over. The new machines weave a hundred times faster and cheaper than I can. Who will come to me for linen anymore?"

Mama was silent for a moment, looking down at the street as they walked home to Opa's house. "But you are dreaming, Ernst. We have no money to go to Texas."

2

A DECISION

That night after Mina had gone to bed, she heard the grownups talking in the big room. She strained to hear what they were saying.

"I love this village, it is my home," Papa said. "But I have no future here, no land, no hope for anything better...."

There was a moment of silence, and then Opa's voice. "*Ja*, my son, it is hard for the second-born. But I have some money put away — enough for you to go to Texas."

Uncle Christian spoke up. "If you give all that money to Ernst, we will have nothing to buy a new wagon."

"You speak of a new wagon, but we speak of a new life, Christian." It was Opa. "Ernst is my son, too. We cannot all live on this farmstead. It is good that he go and seek his fortune elsewhere."

Uncle Christian said something Mina could not hear.

A chair scraped the floor, and Papa shouted. "You will see, Christian, someday you will see."

"Now Ernst, please, sit down." No one spoke for a moment. Then Mama's voice again. "Ernst, we could use your father's money to buy land here."

"No, Minchen, we could not buy enough land with that money anywhere but in Texas where land is still plentiful and cheap. Texas is a Godsend for us — the answer to my prayers."

"Well, my children, you do not have to decide tonight. Let us sleep on it. You have a week to make up your minds."

Mina lay in bed next to Christine thinking about Texas.

"Christine, are you asleep?"

There was no answer except the slow, even breathing of sleep.

Mina wanted to talk to someone. She did not like it when Papa and Uncle Christian argued. She turned her thoughts to Texas. What a fine house they would have. It would be made of stone — three stories high — with a slate roof. And they would have a carriage like the rich people in Bad Salzdetfurth. In the garden there would be orange and banana trees.

In the next days, all the talk was about going to Texas. The more they talked, the more possible it seemed. Mina could hardly sit still in school for thinking about crossing the ocean in a tall sailing ship to live in a paradise.

So when Papa asked one evening, "Do you want to go to Texas, Mina?", she replied without hesitating, "Oh, *ja*, Papa, I do!"

Then Papa's face became very serious — in harmony

with his sad eyes. "Do you realize, Mina, that we will never return here?"

Mina had not thought about that. The word "never" was so final that she could not understand it. Still, she said, "*Ja*, Papa, but other people we know are going too."

Papa nodded his head. Everyone in the room was silent. Papa looked over at Mama. "What do you say, Minchen?"

Mama smiled at him. "I say, let us go, if that is what you want, Ernst."

Suddenly Papa jumped up. "Then . . . we *will* go!"

Mama ran to Papa, and he wrapped his arms around both Mama and Mina. "We *will* go," he repeated. They rocked back and forth locked in Papa's arms.

Summer came, and there was much to be done before leaving for Texas. Boxes had to be made for packing, clothes had to be sewn, dishes carefully packed in straw — a thousand jobs.

On the day before departure Opa presented Papa the little wooden wall clock with *Edelweiss* painted around its face. Mina's great-grandfather had brought it from the Black Forest many years ago. She loved its delicate chiming, and wondered where — in what room — it would resume its ticking and chiming.

At last everything was packed into wooden boxes and loaded onto the *Leiterwagen*, ready for Opa to drive them to Linden where they would board a riverboat for Bremerhaven.

When morning came Mina realized that this was the last time to awaken in the small cozy room she shared with Christine. She looked up at the wooden canopy over the bed. Never again would she open her eyes and look at the cluster of flowers that Opa had carved there.

"Mina, I am sorry you are leaving." Christine turned in the soft feather bed to face her. "This room will seem so quiet without you."

Mina wished Christine had not said that. Now she was not so sure she wanted to leave.

"I know, Christine," Tears started in Mina's eyes. She threw back the covers, and put her feet on the cold wooden floor.

Her doll, Johanna, was lying on top of a trunk in the corner of the room, staring at the ceiling. Her white china face wore the same smile as always. Mina picked her up. Johanna looked happy to be going to Texas today. Mina smiled back at Johanna, sat her on the trunk, and went downstairs to breakfast. She ran to Opa, sitting at the table, threw her arms around his neck and held tightly. His grizzled beard was rough on her cheek.

"Well, how is my Texas girl?" Opa asked.

Mina could not say anything, smiled at Opa, and tried to swallow the lump in her throat, but it would not go away. She did not want to leave Opa and his big warm house that smelled of baking bread and coffee. The early morning sun shone through casement windows onto the dark wooden floor. Schnurri, the cat, lay curled in a square of warm sunshine, her long fur glistening. Mina kneeled down to smooth her fur. Schnurri raised her head to look at Mina, and then began to purr.

"Come, Mina, I will braid your hair." Mama combed out Mina's bangs and long blond hair. Then she parted it down the middle, made two braids, and tied each with a blue ribbon. "There now."

Aunt Sophie called Christine to come to breakfast, and when the whole family was gathered, Opa blessed

9

the food. It was the last time to hear Opa's blessing and eat at this big family table, Mina thought. On the table were thick slices of dark rye bread, an oval mold of yellow butter, steaming mugs of coffee, and a pitcher of warm milk. But Mina was not hungry. It was as though her throat closed up whenever she took a bite.

"Mina, eat your breakfast now. We have a long journey ahead." Mama adjusted one of the bows on her braids.

"I cannot, Mama." She left the table, and went through the hall into the barn where the animals stood in their stalls. In the center of the barn the *Leiterwagen* was waiting. Mina went to the stall where Liesel, the spotted milk cow, watched her with big sad eyes.

"Farewell, Liesel." Mina ran her hand down from the white spot between Liesel's ears along her silky black face, over and over again.

Opa and Papa came in to hitch the horses to the wagon.

"Mina, go and get your things, and do not forget Johanna." Papa climbed in the wagon with Opa, and they drove out into the street to the front of the house.

As Mina came out the front door, she saw that family and friends had gathered to bid them farewell. She ran to Auntie Fischer.

"*Auf Wiedersehen*, Mina." Auntie Fischer wrapped her arms around Mina.

Tightness gripped Mina's throat again. "Farewell, *Tante*."

Someone touched Mina's shoulder gently. "Good-bye, Mina." It was Christine. They embraced one another. "How I shall miss you."

"Oh, Christine, you have been like a sister. We shall

see each other again someday." But Mina knew in her heart that day would never be.

Papa shook hands with Uncle Christian, kissed Aunt Sophie and then Christine.

"*Lebe wohl*, Uncle Ernst," Christine said, "I will write to you."

Papa, Mama, and Mina climbed into the wagon with Opa, and he clucked at the team of horses. The wagon lurched forward, and that seemed to loosen the sobs Mina had been holding back. She buried her face on Papa's shoulder as she heard, "*Auf Wiedersehen*. God be with you."

Mina looked back through blurry eyes. The group of people, all waving, was growing smaller. Cousin Hans ran after the wagon for a way, then stopped, and he too was left behind. The tears streamed down Mina's cheeks as the wagon rolled out of Wehrstedt, and Papa's arm tightened around her shoulders.

At last the sobs were finished. Mina straightened up and looked back.

"Farewell, Wehrstedt," she called, waving at the sight of the neat village nestled in the valley just below the Ziegenberg. Only the church spire rose above the tree tops. She thought of Hans standing helpless in the middle of the road — helpless to catch them and hold them back.

The road followed a stream, out through a gap in the hills.

"Papa, I hope our new home will be in the hills like these."

"I hope so too, Mina." Papa looked straight ahead.

Opa was silent as he drove the wagon, and there were tears running down Mama's pale cheeks.

Mina took a last look at the wooded hills. Then she turned around, flipped her braid over her shoulder, and never looked back again.

3

LAST DAYS IN GERMANY

At Linden they said farewell for the last time to Opa. Mina would never forget Opa's face as he stood on the pier. Tears glistened in his eyes and ran down his cheeks to hide in his beard. Mina waved and waved as the riverboat pulled slowly away. Then a bend in the river separated them forever.

Toward the end of the day, they put in at Verden. Men slept out on deck while women and small children slept on benches inside the deck house. The bench was narrow and hard, but Mina finally fell asleep using her coat for a pillow.

In the morning some more passengers boarded, and the boat continued down river. Before long they had reached the place where the Leine flows into the Weser River which grew wider and wider as the boat neared Bremen.

The deck was so crowded with people and their belongings that Mina climbed up on a box to see the passing shoreline. She held onto Papa's shoulder with one hand to steady herself. Up ahead Mina saw the roofs and spires of a great city beside the river.

Closer and closer to Bremen they came until the boat pulled alongside a pier.

"Come, Mina, get down, for we may bump."

Two crewmen jumped onto the pier, and hastened to tie the boat, fore and aft. People from other riverboats were milling about on the pier.

"Well, we have an hour's stop here before going on to Bremerhaven." Papa took Mina's hand, and put his other arm on Mama's shoulder. "Come, let us take a walk and see the city."

"Papa, I want to see the statue of Roland."

"Very well, Ernst, but someone must watch our belongings." Mama got up from her seat on a box.

"*Ja*, Minchen, I will ask *Frau* Müller over there."

When Papa had arranged everything, they stepped onto the pier and walked along the street. People hurried along on foot until a carriage passed, scattering them in its wake.

The street led into the market square which was surrounded by tall stone buildings. Mina counted seven stories in one of them. But most amazing of all was the giant statue of Roland — at least two stories tall — standing before the City Hall. He had a shield over his left shoulder, and held a broadsword on his right.

Mina caught her breath. Roland looked so heroic. She imagined his holding the sword aloft and saying, "Never surrender — stand and fight to the end." He had fought until all his men fell, and he too was mortally wounded. Then she heard him blow his enchanted horn. Its clear piercing melody floated over the mountains,

14

finally reaching the ears of his uncle, the Emperor Charlemagne, sitting in his war tent. But when Charlemagne came with his army to help, Roland lay dead, his face turned toward the fleeing enemy.

So lost was Mina in her thoughts that it startled her when Papa said, "It is time to get back." Papa took her hand, and they started toward the river. Mina felt herself being pulled along as she looked this way and that. She could not get enough of all the city sights.

It was only a short walk to the pier. They made their way through other passengers to where their boxes were.

Mama sighed. "My, it feels good to sit down."

But Mina was not tired. She watched the men cast off from the pier, and a black puff of smoke came out of the smokestack. As they pulled away, the ancient city of Bremen began to slip into the distance.

Daylight was fading when they docked at Bremerhaven and stepped onto the cobblestoned quay. Great ships lined the long quay as far as Mina could see. On the closest ship sailors were taking their ease on deck lighted by lanterns that swung to and fro. Above them rose the skeletal masts and yardarms. Water lapped and splashed on the hull, and somewhere a sailor played a harmonica.

"Which one is the *Margaretha*, Papa?"

"We will see tomorrow, Mina."

15

That night they spent in a building that opened right onto the quay — a warehouse the *Adelsverein* provided for its members. It was just one huge room where everyone slept on cots.

In the morning Mina was awake early. She had slept only fitfully. For one thing she was uncomfortable sleeping in her clothes, and for another there had been a chorus of snoring all night. Besides it was hard to wait to see the *Margaretha* when she knew the ship was right outside along the quay somewhere, waiting for her.

The *Adelsverein* served coffee from a table set up at one end of the room. After some bread and cheese that Mama had brought along, Mina finally got Papa out the door and into the warm sunshine on the quay. It was a wide walkway with bobbing ships on one side, and substantial stone buildings on the other.

Even being so wide the quay was congested with people and their boxed belongings waiting to board ships. Mina danced along holding Papa's hand. In his other hand Papa held his long stemmed pipe, and the smoke trailed behind as they walked along.

Mina looked at the stern of each ship for the name. There were the *Ida*, the *Hercules*, the *America*. About halfway along the quay they came to a two masted brig, and on its stern was painted *Margaretha* between two circular flower designs.

"Papa!" Mina caught her breath, "there she is." Mina's heart leaped within her chest, and she began to pull Papa closer to the rocking ship.

The *Margaretha* was not the biggest ship docked at the quay, but she was not the smallest by any means. And after the river steamer she looked grand to Mina. On her bow just beneath the bowsprit was a wooden figure-head of a lady in a long flowing blue-green dress

16

the color of the sea. Her blond hair rippled down her back in lovely waves. In one hand was a cross which she held over her breast. Her head was held high as she surveyed the horizon.

Sailors were busy at various jobs — painting the deck, repairing sails and rigging, making the *Margaretha* ready for the long voyage.

Three days passed, and at last the Captain sent word that passengers should board. Tomorrow at dawn they would *sail.* The very word sent a tremor through Mina's body.

Papa, Mama, and Mina hauled and pushed their boxes one by one up the ramp and onto the deck of the *Margaretha.*

"I cannot go another step, Ernst, without resting."

"*Ja,* Minchen, you and Mina rest here on the boxes we need for the voyage. I will see to getting these others stored in the hold."

"Let me go with you, Papa."

"*Nein,* Mina, you stay with Mama."

Mina plopped down on a box with a sigh. She did not want to sit at such an exciting time. She flipped her braids over her shoulders, and swung her feet out to the side and back, bumping her shoes together with a snap. She watched as other passengers struggled up the ramp with their boxes.

When Papa returned, the three of them carried their boxes down the narrow stepway below deck to steerage where their living quarters were to be. Coming from the sunny deck into steerage was like day into night.

"But it is so dark in here," Mina complained.

There were no windows, and the only light came in through the doorways at either end of the big room. Once

17

her eyes got accustomed to it she could see that the walls were lined with compartments of four berths each. They were open to the central space. People were busy in some of them rolling out mattresses and making beds. In the center of the room was the lower part of the mainmast as it passed down through the ship. A bench circled it, and a lamp hung from a peg on one side.

"Let us take that one over there." Mama pointed to a compartment across the room next to the end wall. "It will be more private."

They pushed the boxes into the space between berths. Mama opened one of them, and took out a blanket.

"Ernst, do you think you could hang this across the opening?"

While Papa hung the blanket, Mina opened a box, and took Johanna out. "We are on our way to Texas, Johanna, and this is our room to live in." Mina set Johanna on a box with her back against the wall.

Mama took off her bonnet. "First we must get our things unpacked. Ernst, take out the mattresses, and we will make the beds."

After the beds were made, and Johanna was resting comfortably on Mina's upper berth, they began to unpack the tin dishes. Mama hung the cups and the coffee pot from pegs in the beam overhead. They arranged the boxes to make a table and two benches between berths. Before long the compartment looked comfortable.

"There." Mama sat down with a satisfied sigh. She looked pale. The work had tired her out.

"Mama, you must rest now."

Just then Mina heard the cook calling from the galley above, "Supper is ready."

"I will get your supper, Mama." Mina picked up three bowls and gave one to Papa.

There was already a long line waiting outside the galley. When at last Papa and Mina reached the galley door, the cook filled their bowls with peas and bits of pork. Then when they were back in the compartment, Mama took out a loaf of bread and cut some slices. The pork was dry and tough, but Mina was too hungry to mind. After they had eaten Mama seemed to feel better.

That night Mina crawled into her upper berth, and snuggled Johanna next to her. She could hear other families talking in their compartments, and sometimes children crying. Next door was the Kaufmann family who came from Armstedt, a village near Wehrstedt. Anna, their daughter, was ten years old also, and *Frau* Kaufmann was expecting a baby in early January.

Mina tapped on the thin partition that separated them from the Kaufmanns. "Anna, are you in your berth?"

"*Ja*, Mina." Anna tapped back. "My berth is right next to yours."

"Good, we can send messages to each other."

"Go to sleep, Mina," Papa said. "We will be up early in the morning."

Mina took a deep breath, relaxed, and let the *Margaretha* rock her gently to and fro. It was like being a baby in a cradle — really very comforting — and slowly she felt herself being lulled to sleep inside the great ship.

4

THE STORM

Mina awoke to the sound of heavy stomping over-head. She could not think where she was. Her bed was rocking back and forth, back and forth. Then Mina opened her eyes. A dim light filtered into the small compartment. Close above her were rough planks of the ceiling — not the delicately carved flowers of her own bed. She was on the *Margaretha*, and this morning they sailed at dawn.

On deck above her head sailors were up and about, shouting to each other. Mina could not stay in bed any longer.

"Papa, Mama, wake up, we are about to leave." Mina dressed quickly.

Papa chuckled. "Well, Minchen, there will be no peace until we get up."

Mama yawned and stretched in the berth below Mina's.

"Hurry, or we will miss everything." Mina climbed

down from the berth to put on her shoes. "May I go up on deck to watch?"

"*Nein*, Mina, you wait for us," Mama said getting out of bed. "Go sit on the bench."

Mina went out through the curtain, sat down heavily, and leaned against the mast. The light coming in through the doorways was growing brighter. Any minute now the sun would rise, the *Margaretha* would sail, and Mina would miss it all, sitting and waiting down in steerage.

Finally Mama pulled aside the curtain, and they all went up on deck and stood at the rail. Mina looked at the line that held the *Margaretha* to the quay. As she rocked, the line became taut and loose. It seemed to Mina that the ship was pulling on the line, anxious to be on her way across the great ocean. Mina looked up at the two towering masts — their yards strung with a maze of lines. The sails were still furled.

On the quarter deck Captain Libben stood with his hands clasped behind his back, looking aloft. He was a stout man with a gray beard and mustache, and he wore a black billed cap squarely on his head. He watched as his sailors climbed up the rigging to the yardarms. On either side of him stood the pilot and the First Mate.

Then Captain Libben gave the command to the First Mate who shouted, "Loose the topsails." Mina saw the square sails unfurl, flap, and fill with wind as the sailors turned the big winches to trim them.

"Heave ho," sang the men cranking up the anchor. The ship steadied, and began to cut smoothly through the water with the wind.

"Oh, Papa, we are moving!" The quay and all the waving people on it were slipping away. The *Margaretha* glided slowly past a forest of masts and rigging of the

21

other ships. Sailors on these ships stopped their work and waved as the *Margaretha* sailed by, and Mina waved back. The wind pushed them out into the wide harbor, away from other ships, away from Bremerhaven.

Papa and Mama put their arms around Mina's shoulders. Mina looked up at Papa. His eyes were sad as he gazed toward the flat coastline.

"Are you thinking of Opa?" Mina asked.

"*Ja, kleine* Mina, and of Germany. We shall never set eyes on our Fatherland again."

Mama watched as the harbor grew farther and farther away. "*Auf Wiedersehen,* our Fatherland," she cried raising her arm to wave, her long skirt blowing in the breeze.

For Mina, leaving Bremerhaven was not as hard as leaving Opa and their big house in Wehrstedt. Back there she felt that something inside her was being torn out, leaving her cold and numb. But now she felt only a surge of excitement through her body.

"*Auf Wiedersehen,*" repeated Mina, "we are off to the new land."

Papa smiled down at her. He looked so fine in his long black coat.

"*Ja,* my *kleine* Mina, you are right. We must be glad, not sad, for we are on our way to Texas and our new life."

Mina turned her face into the fresh seabreeze, and bounced up on her toes. "Oh, Papa, I am so excited. Will it really be like paradise in Texas?"

"That is what they say, Mina."

Mama clasped her hands together. "Just think, our very own land to farm!"

Mina watched as the flat coastline disappeared over the horizon, until all she could see in every direction was the gray restless ocean. Germany was gone forever.

One night after Mina was settled in her berth, the wind began to blow harder and harder until it was howling. She could hear the waves beat against the hull of the ship at her head. The ship began to roll back and forth. Every box in steerage was sliding this way and that. The tin dishes flew about, clanging and rattling. Some of the children began to cry. Mina's stomach felt queasy, and she hugged Johanna close.

"Ernst," Mama called to Papa, "I feel sick." Papa held a chamber pot beside her berth.

"It will be all right, Minchen," Papa assured her.

But as the ship rolled more violently, Mina held onto the side of her berth. One moment she felt she was standing on her head, the next moment on her feet.

"Papa, Papa, the waves will turn us over!"

"*Nein*, Mina." Papa's voice was strong and sure. "This is a sturdy ship, and Captain Libben knows his business."

She heard Anna cry out in the next compartment, "Papa, we shall drown!"

Mina thought of the angry waves outside. She imagined herself bobbing about in the dark water, trying to keep her head up.

Then a wave dashed against the hull, bringing Mina out of her vision. It hit so hard that the *Margaretha* seemed to stop, and with a shudder, heeled over until Mina thought they would capsize.

People screamed and cried out in the dark, "Dear God, help us, help us."

The ship righted herself, and rolled in the opposite direction. Mina clung to her berth with both hands to keep from being thrown against the hull or onto the floor.

"Papa, I wish I was home in Wehrstedt. I wish we had never come on this terrible ship. I hate it, Papa, I hate it. I want to go home." Mina felt the warm tears running down her cheeks, and she was shaking all over.

"You must be brave, my *kleine* Mina, and trust in God." Papa reached over and held onto Mina's hand. His hand was rough and warm.

The *Margaretha* bucked and rolled. Another giant wave slammed into her hull. The sea was trying to pull her down, down into its depths. The *Margaretha* creaked and groaned as each new wave rolled her over.

Another wave, and another, pounding, pounding on the ship's sides. Only a thin wall separated them from the raging, foaming ocean.

"Ernst, you must pray to God to save us."

"Our God in heaven," Papa began, and his voice encircled them with its strength. "Help us through this night, and give us courage to help ourselves." The waves continued to pound the *Margaretha*, but Mina relaxed her grip on the berth.

She felt ashamed that she had been such a baby. She thought of Captain Libben and his helmsman at the wheel guiding the ship through the storm. She thought of the blond lady on the bow cutting bravely through the water, and of Papa's words, "give us courage to help our-

25

selves." I want to be brave like Captain Libben and Papa and Roland, thought Mina.

At last dawn came. The wind was still blowing, but not as hard. Mina could hear the pump throbbing as it pumped out water that had leaked in during the storm. She opened her eyes and looked about the dimly lit compartment. Their boxes had shifted, and there were no cups left on the pegs above her head. Her dress and shoes were safely tucked into the space between her berth and the wall. Mina pulled her dress on over her head, put on her high top shoes, and buttoned them.

Papa came in through the curtain, and Mama stirred.

"Minchen, just stay in bed for awhile. The storm is over, and you will soon feel better."

Then the cook's voice from above, "Coffee is ready."

"Come, Mina, let us find our coffee pot and cups." Papa helped her jump down from the berth, and together they began to pick through the clutter on the floor of the big room. Other passengers were stirring about, picking up belongings.

"Aha, here is the pot." Papa found it under the bench that circled the mast.

They climbed the steps, and went out onto the deck. The sky had cleared and the sun felt warm on Mina's face. The ship creaked as it rolled, but Mina knew now that it was strong. She looked up at Papa and took his hand.

Papa smiled at her. "I told you, *kleine* Mina, that this was a sturdy ship. And more than that, you are a sturdy girl."

Mina straightened her back, and stood up tall.

5

THE LONG PASSAGE

The *Margaretha* began to seem like Mina's home. It was almost as if she had known no other all her life. Day after day passed, and Mina grew tired of being confined on a ship in the middle of the ocean. Once in awhile something happened which made that day different from the sameness of all the others.

Mina was drying the breakfast dishes one morning as Mama washed them in a bucket of sea water. The curtain to their compartment was open, and she saw the younger children playing on the floor. Some were chasing each other this way and that, bumping into grownups.

Anna appeared, her dark brown hair neatly braided. "Mina, are you ready to go up on deck?"

"*Ja*, Anna, almost." Mina hurriedly dried and put away the last tin dish. "Mama, may I go now?"

"Sure, Mina, but do not get in the sailors' way."

They went up the steps and onto the clean white plank deck which had just been scrubbed. Many of the

27

grownups were taking their morning stroll about the deck, including Captain Libben.

"Good morning, young ladies." He touched the bill of his cap with his hand.

"Good morning, Captain Libben." Mina thought he looked the master of the ship.

It was a fine day with a steady breeze filling the sails without a ripple. Sailors were at work repairing lines and rigging.

Mina's eyes swept across the wavy sea. Suddenly a fish leaped out of the water, making an arc with its body as it dived back down.

"Anna, Anna, look there!" Mina pointed out to sea. More fish leaped out of the water until the sea was alive with glistening black arcs.

"A school of dolphins." Captain Libben stood at the rail smoking his pipe. "Smartest creature in the sea." And he took another puff, leaning his elbows on the rail.

"Captain Libben, do you know all the fish in the sea?" Mina asked.

"Well, *Fräulein*, not every one personally." He straightened up and chuckled at his own joke. "But the dolphin is one I would dearly like to befriend. Yes, indeed."

Mina giggled and watched the dolphins frolic. "It would be exciting to ride on the back of one of those dolphins."

"Mina! the things you think of. Why it makes me shudder just to imagine it," Anna exclaimed.

Mina enjoyed Anna's astonishment. But she really felt that tug on her to try things, to test herself. At school in Wehrstedt she was the only girl who would dare to jump out the window into the snow, much to the horror of little Angelica, the school's curly haired angel. How dull to be an angel.

28

The days were long, and one faded into another. Sometimes it was rainy and cold, and Mina and Anna could not go on deck. Then Papa would take out the books he had brought along for Mina. Anna came for lessons too.

Papa had a map of the world, and once a week he let Mina or Anna draw a ship on the ocean where they were. Mina looked at North America and the place where they would make their home in Texas. She tried to imagine what that place was like. Were there big trees with bright green parrots on the branches and monkeys swinging from limb to limb?

"I wish the wind would hurry up and blow us to Texas," Mina said. "I am tired of being on this ship."

"But not *too* fast." Anna's eyes suddenly looked worried. "I do not think I could stand another storm with all that rocking back and forth, and thinking any minute we would be thrown into the ocean." Anna put her hands to her breast as if to still her heart.

"Oh, Anna, do not be such a baby. Captain Libben knows his business." Still, Mina hoped there would not be another night like that either.

Day after day Mina watched the ocean — sometimes sparkling in the sun, other times dark and rolling under a cloudy sky. Then, she saw another ship, small on the horizon. She ran to find Papa, and they watched as it came closer. A flag went up — the three striped red, white, and blue flag of France. Shortly the sailors hoisted the *Margaretha's* flag — a silver horse on a red background.

As the two ships came directly across from each

other, Mina saw on its deck two sailors holding a large chalkboard with this written on it:

61°15'

Lat 27°N

"What does it mean, Papa?" Mina asked.

"Those numbers tell the exact place on the ocean where the other Captain thinks we are, according to his navigation," Papa explained.

Immediately two of the *Margaretha's* sailors came on deck with a board on which were also written large numbers. They held it up for the passing ship to see.

"Our Captain is answering," said Papa, "and his calculations are almost the same."

It must be exciting to be a captain, thought Mina, and guide your ship across this great markless ocean, navigating only by the sun and stars. If only girls could do all the adventurous things that boys could. But whoever heard of a girl captain? Or a girl soldier? It was not fair, really.

September passed, and October also. Finally in November Captain Libben said that land would be seen any day now.

"Tonight we shall have a dance on deck," the Captain announced. "So bring your musical instruments, and have a merry time."

"Papa, you can play your harmonica!" Mina jumped up and down.

The evening was warm with only a gentle breeze. The *Margaretha* plowed through the water while on her decks the passengers danced. Mina wore her best blue dress and let her long golden hair hang loose. A fat man played an accordion. His stomach was so rounded he could hardly reach the keys, and the accordion bounced when he played. Papa played his harmonica and danced at the same time. Mama looked so pretty and young, almost like a girl herself. Though her long dress was dark, her skin and hair glowed in the moonlight. They all danced — the young and old together while the full moon shone down on them. Mina thought she had never been so happy.

Every morning Mina got up earlier than Papa and Mama, and went up on deck to look for land. One morning as she searched the horizon, Mina heard the words ring out.

"Land! Land, ho," shouted a sailor from aloft the foremast.

Mina looked in the direction he was pointing. There, almost like a shadow on the horizon, Mina saw mountains.

She turned quickly, and ran to tell Mama and Papa. They were already coming up the ladder. Passengers erupted onto the deck, and lined the railing to see land.

Mina knew from her geography lessons that this must be the island of Santo Domingo or Haiti. There would still be weeks to go, but land was in sight. And it would not be long until they reached Texas.

6

TEXAS AT LAST

As the *Margaretha* sailed closer to the coast of Texas seagulls flew about overhead. Mina marveled at the way they seemed to float almost motionless above her. She loved the seagulls' cries, for it meant land was near.

Mama came on deck and stood beside Mina. She had a ship's biscuit to feed the gulls.

"Here, Mina." Mama broke the biscuit and gave Mina half. Then Mama held out a piece of biscuit for the gulls as high as she could reach. Mina threw pieces into the water, and watched as the gulls swooped down to get the bread.

At last a brave gull flew down close to them, and hovered a few minutes. Mama was very still. The gull swooped down and took the biscuit from Mama's fingers.

"Oh, Mama! He flew so close."

"*Ja*, Mina, I wish I could fly like the gulls — so graceful in the wind, so free. I would fly right up to the heavens." Mama looked longingly upward, her cheeks flushed with excitement.

Mama and Mina had been busy washing and packing clothes, getting ready for arrival in Galveston. It was the end of November when Galveston was sighted early in the morning. Passengers crowded on deck to watch as the *Margaretha* came closer and closer to the flat coastal island.

"Galveston is only a village." Mina pointed toward the island. "I thought it was the biggest city in Texas."

"That it is, Mina, but Texas is young, and Galveston is only eight years old. Give it a little time to grow, like a child." Papa patted Mina on the shoulder.

"How long will we stay in Galveston, Papa?"

"Not long, for we will take another boat along the coast to Indian Point."

Sailors scurried here and there preparing the *Margaretha* to anchor just outside the harbor. Captain Libben gave the order to the First Mate who shouted, "Let out the sails." And then, "Drop anchor." The sails flapped loosely in the wind until sailors climbed the rigging and began to furl them. The anchor went clanking down, down into the sea. The *Margaretha* rocked gently on the waves.

"Are we going to stop out here in the ocean, Ernst?" asked Mama.

"*Ja*, Minchen, Captain Libben said the harbor is not deep enough for large ships."

Some flat barges came out of the harbor rowing toward the *Margaretha*.

33

"Well, now we must bring our boxes on deck so we can be lightered ashore."

Down below everyone was busy moving boxes.

Anna appeared at the Jordans' compartment. "Can you believe we are here, Mina, after so long?"

"Oh, Anna, I can hardly wait. Just think, we shall soon step onto Texas!"

The two girls joined hands and danced around in a circle amid the pushing and sliding of boxes.

Then stopping, Anna looked at Mina closely with a worried expression. "What do you think it will be like?"

"Well . . . it will be solid, that is one thing for sure."

"I mean, do you think there will be any of those Indians?" Her eyes were big.

"Oh, Anna, I do believe if you ever see an Indian you will faint away like some fine lady."

"I will *not*. You think you are so brave, Mina. I wonder what *you* will do if an Indian comes?"

"Why, I will just throw my arms around him and give him a big hug, Anna." Mina tossed her braids, and looked at Anna. As soon as she said those words and saw the hurt expression on Anna's face, she was sorry she said them. Words tumbled out of her mouth before she had a chance to think them over. But Anna could be so fearful, so timid sometimes that it made Mina impatient with her.

"Come, Mina, we need your help," Mama called after she and Papa had closed the last box. Mina and Mama took one handle while Papa carried the other end of the heavy box up the ladder.

They set the box on deck which was now crowded with boxes and belongings. Mama was out of breath, and sat down for a moment to rest. Sailors were bringing boxes that had been stored in the hold.

The wide flat barges had reached the side of the *Margaretha*. Mina looked down at them clustered about, waiting to carry passengers and cargo into the harbor. Steep wooden steps had been lowered to one of the barges, and the first passengers began to leave the *Margaretha* carrying their belongings, the men lowering heavy boxes.

Soon it was the Jordans' turn to leave. Mina took one last look at the *Margaretha*'s deck, and waved goodbye to Captain Libben.

"So long, Miss, and good luck in your new home." The Captain touched the bill of his cap in salute.

"Goodbye, Captain Libben. Thank you for a safe voyage." Mina started down the steps. She held Johanna tightly in the crook of her arm.

The barge tipped as it was loaded, and the boatman warned them, "Sit down quickly, folks, and do not move about, or we shall have to swim to Galveston." Mina sat, and looked up at the ship's rail, now high above her. Anna appeared at the rail.

"I will see you in Galveston," Mina called, waving. She wished she had not been so mean to Anna.

As they rowed into the harbor Mina could hardly sit still. The water was quieter inside the harbor. Long piers reached out from land, and they tied up at one of these, and began to unload.

Mina stepped out of the barge and onto the pier.

How strange! When she stood on the pier it seemed to be rocking back and forth like a ship. She ran to Papa who had just gotten their boxes out of the barge.

"Papa, I am still swaying."

Papa laughed. "I, too, Mina."

"Oh, my!" Mama was holding onto Papa's arm. "I feel I am still rocking on the waves."

A man who had been standing on the pier walked over to Papa. "Welcome to Texas. I am D. H. Klaener, agent for the *Adelsverein,* or simply the *Verein* as we call it here."

"How do you do?" Papa reached out his hand, and they shook.

The agent greeted others as they stepped onto the pier.

"Well, now that you are all here, we must see to moving these boxes. The *Verein* has rented quarters for you to stay here a few days until the steamer leaves for Indian Point." *Herr* Klaener turned and looked about him. "So, if you men will come with me, we will get some wheelbarrows." He started walking along the pier toward land.

"Let me go, too, Papa," begged Mina, dancing about.

"Very well." Papa turned to Mama. "We shall return soon, Minchen."

"All right, Ernst." Mama sat down. "I will stay here and watch the boxes."

Mina and Papa walked the long pier over marshy land into Galveston. Mina skipped along holding Papa's hand.

The broad sandy street was crowded with people. Mina heard Americans speaking English. It sounded strange, and she could not understand a word.

36

All the buildings were made of wood. There were no stone buildings like those back in Germany. Up ahead on the left was a two-story wooden building with porch galleries all around. It was the Hotel Meyer.

The *Verein* had rented several vacant buildings. Though not as comfortable looking as the Hotel Meyer, they were at least shelter. Several families had to crowd into each room, and cooking had to be done outside.

After moving the boxes, and settling into one of the rooms with the Kaufmann family, Papa and Mina went to a store they had seen on the main street—Kretzer and Maerz, Dealers in Hardware.

Inside, the storekeeper greeted them in German, "*Guten Tag.*"

"*Guten Tag.*" Papa nodded his head. "We are on our way to Indian Point and the German colony in a few days, and I am looking at tools."

"Well, if you are going inland, I would advise you to purchase a gun."

Mina looked up at Papa. "What do we need a gun for, Papa?"

"Well, *Fräulein,* your Papa can use it to hunt, and to protect the family from Indians." Then, lowering his voice, he spoke some words to Papa that Mina overheard. "You know, two German settlers were killed and scalped last month near Austin."

Scalped! The word sent a shot of terror through Mina. She imagined herself walking through the woods when suddenly from behind a tree jumped an Indian. His white eyeballs glowed fiercely in his dark face. His arm was raised, and in his hand was a tomahawk. Mina shivered. She did not know what she would do if she ever saw an Indian.

Papa went over to the rack of guns hung on the back

37

wall. "What kind of gun would you suggest? I have no experience with firearms."

"Then a shotgun would be best for you, because it does not require such careful aim." The shopkeeper took down a double barreled shotgun and showed it to Papa.

Papa looked at the gun carefully, turning it this way and that. Then he handed it back to the shopkeeper. "Very well, I will come back tomorrow."

When they returned to the *Adelsverein* house Mama and *Frau* Kaufmann were cooking over an open fire.

"Mama, we are going to buy a gun to protect us from Indians!"

Mama looked at Papa with a question in her eyes.

"It will be a good idea, Minchen. After all, this is the frontier. We may never see an unfriendly Indian, but in case we do . . ."

"Oh, Ernst, I do not like guns."

"Nor do I, Minchen."

"But, Ernst, our land is not in Indian territory, is it?"

"Surely not," Papa answered. "I will probably never need the gun for protection, but just in case."

It was the "just in case" that sent a shiver through Mina.

That evening the Jordans and Kaufmanns sat around on boxes in their small room to eat dinner. Mina folded her hands in her lap, and bowed her head as Papa began his blessing of the food.

Our God in Heaven,   Bless our families,
We thank Thee   And all those who
For a safe voyage   Come here with hope
And this good food.   In their hearts
Bless our new land.   For a new life.
                                              Amen.

7

A LONELY COAST

For three days the coastal steamer chugged along the flat coast of Texas, black smoke pouring out of its smokestack. Two giant paddlewheels on either side of the steamer splashed noisily pushing her through the water, and the two square sails fore and aft filled with the easterly wind.

Mina was hungry. The only food on the ship was bread and warm water for coffee. Mama had bought some provisions in Galveston, but Mina longed for a cup of milk and some cheese to go with the bread.

"Papa, will there be food for us when we get to Indian Point?"

"*Ja*, sure, Mina." He was sitting on a box cleaning his shotgun. "The *Verein* will have a place for us to eat and stay the night."

Mina liked this shiny new gun of Papa's with the polished wooden stock. She ran her finger along the cold smooth barrels. No Indian would bother them with such a protector.

"Papa, could you teach me to shoot your gun?"

Papa stopped cleaning and looked at Mina. "Now, my *kleine* Mina, whatever would you need to shoot a gun for?" There was a hint of a smile on the right side of his wide mouth.

"Well, Papa, suppose there was an Indian who was not friendly, and suppose you were out in the field somewhere. What would Mama and I do?" Mina waited a moment to see if Papa would say something, but he just looked at Mina with a sort of sad, faraway look in his eyes. Then he took a deep breath.

"Very well, Mina, I will show you." He handed the gun to Mina, and she put the wooden stock against her right shoulder and looked down the barrels squinting her left eye. She aimed toward the ship's rail.

"Now, find something to steady your aim, Mina."

She knelt beside one of their boxes, and put her arm on top.

"Pull the hammer back to full cock and center the front sight."

With the constant motion of the ship it was hard to hold the bead in the center.

"I have it, Papa."

"All right, now, squeeze the front trigger slowly."

Mina squeezed, and the hammer clicked against the cap.

"When we are on shore I will show you how to load it, Mina."

What would little Angelica do if she knew Mina was learning to fire a shotgun. The thought of the look on her face made Mina giggle.

In the afternoon a cold wind began to blow from the

41

north as the steamer entered Matagorda Bay. It was a flat empty coastline — no trees, no houses. Mina, Papa, and Mama stood with the Kaufmanns watching this lonely coastline. Mina was warmly bundled with a woolen scarf on her head.

Suddenly, around a bend in the distance Mina saw people on the beach, and an assortment of tents.

"Papa, Papa, look." Mina pointed toward the beach.

"Indian Point," a sailor cried out.

"Those people must be Germans from other ships," said Papa.

"But why are there so many?" Mina looked up at him for an answer.

"Ernst, what does it mean?" Mama asked.

"Now, Minchen, do not fret. We may have to camp here for a day or two, but everything will be all right." Papa's face had a worried look as though he did not really believe his own words.

As they drew near the beach in the row boat, Mina snuggled between Papa and Mama. Johanna was buttoned inside her coat. People gathered at the landing spot, watching solemnly. The boat's bow ran up onto the beach, and the oarsman jumped out and pulled it further onto land.

"We sure do not need anymore hungry Germans here," a grim faced man shouted.

"Oh, be quiet, Herman," said another.

"He is right, of course. You will go back to Germany if you know what is good for you."

Mina looked at the group gathered on the beach. Their faces were haggard. She pulled her coat more tightly around her.

"Come, come now. What kind of welcome is that?" asked a man who began to help unload the boxes.

When the unloading was finished Papa shook hands with the kind man. "Many thanks. I am Ernst Jordan from Wehrstedt, and this is my wife, and my daughter, Mina."

"My name is Peter Bauer from Ebstorf." He put his other hand over Papa's as they shook. "Maybe we should all have stayed back in Germany."

"What has happened?" asked Papa. "Where is the *Verein*?"

"Ah, well, we do not know," *Herr* Bauer said with a deep sigh. "A month we have been here, and no wagons have come to carry us inland. It is not good."

Mina looked around at the camp. The tents were lonely and drab, flapping in the wind. Some were merely bedspreads or tablecloths stretched over branches.

"Papa, I want to go home to Germany. I do not like Texas." But she knew with a sinking feeling that they could not go back.

"You know we cannot go back to Germany. So, first we shall make a shelter, and then we shall see."

Somehow Papa's words made Mina feel better, more hopeful.

Herr Bauer loaned Papa a shovel and helped them dig a rectangular hole in the ground. Mina and Mama packed the dirt into low walls.

"Well, there is one thing to be thankful for," said *Herr* Bauer. "We have fresh meat for the catching—fish, turtles, prairie chicken. You will become a hunter very quickly, *Herr* Jordan." He chuckled.

Papa stopped digging for a moment. "*Ja*, you see, Minchen, it is a good thing I bought the shotgun."

Mama did not reply, but went on packing the walls.

43

It was nearly dark by the time they covered it over with brush and small branches. Mama took out the gray blanket that had hung across the compartment in the *Margaretha*. It now became the roof of the dugout.

Mina had to crawl inside like a wild animal. It was dark and damp, but at least out of the wind.

"Minchen, do we still have some food in the box?" Papa asked.

"*Ja*, Ernst, we have dried fruit and ship's biscuits. But not much."

"Then that will have to do." Papa turned to Mina. "Tomorrow Mina and I will catch some fish—somehow."

"But, Ernst, how long must we stay here camped in this hovel?" Mama asked.

"I do not know, Minchen, but God will see us through."

"I knew we should not have come to this wilderness, Ernst. And now, see what misery we have found." Mama put her face in her hands and began to weep silently.

"Minchen, you must do your part. God helps those who help themselves." He put his hand gently on the back of her golden hair.

Mama straightened up suddenly. "I should not have listened to you — that would have been my part!" Her eyes were brimming with tears. "What did you know about Texas? What did anyone know?"

Mina crawled out of the tent and put her hands over her ears. A light rain had begun to fall. She looked along the curving coastline cluttered with the motley tents. There was one small house in the distance — a farmer's house, Mina guessed — and other than that, nothing for as far as she could see but flat land and scattered small ponds.

"Mina," Papa came out of the tent, "come, you must not catch cold. Come inside the tent."

The tent did not look cozy, but there was nowhere else to go. Inside, Mama had spread blankets. Mina lay down on the hard cold ground, and pulled the blankets around her. She wished she were back in Opa's warm, cheery house.

8

CHRISTMAS ON THE BEACH

There were only two days left before Christmas. But how can we have Christmas here? Mina wondered. We have no home, no fir tree, no feast for the table. Christmas could not come to this forlorn beach.

Back home in Germany, Christmas was the best time of the year. The village was blanketed with snow. Inside every house there was a *Tannenbaum* glowing with candles and ornaments. And on every dining table a Christmas feast was spread.

It had been raining every day, soaking their tent until it began to leak. Mama used tin cups to catch as many drips as she could. Whenever the rain stopped Papa and Mina would wring out the blanket, and place it back over the branches.

Mina walked along the beach away from the camp. For once it had stopped raining. She was searching for something to give Papa and Mama for Christmas. Maybe the sea would wash something up.

The grownups did not talk of Christmas. They talked of the lack of food and the sickness that was in almost every tent. And they talked of the cold, rainy weather that made the roads impossible to travel.

"Even if we had wagons and oxen, we could not get through on those roads," *Herr* Kaufmann had said to Papa.

"*Ja*, you are right, Heinrich, we would sink to the axles. We must stay here and wait."

Mina pulled her coat tighter around her to keep out the cold wind, and trudged along. She thought of *Frau* Kaufmann. Her baby would come soon. And they did not even have a decent roof over their heads. She thought of last night when Mama had said, "I wish I had never heard of Texas, Ernst."

Papa's face was so sad that Mina wanted to wrap her arms around his neck and make him smile.

But he just answered, "You must have faith, Minchen. Better times will come."

Mina tried to believe that. Though her stomach always felt empty, and she longed for some milk to drink, she wanted to believe Papa.

Up ahead she saw a small black shell. What luck! It was not broken. She picked it up and turned it over in her hands. A perfectly symmetrical shell that flared like a fan — just the gift for Mama. She put it in her pocket and walked on. Now something for Papa. Mina went closer to the water's edge. There, half buried in the sand, she found a flat white circular shell with a five pointed design on it — like a star.

"The star of Bethlehem! I will give you to Papa,"

Mina said out loud to the shell. She took off her woolen scarf and carefully wrapped it up.

In the morning Mina went to Anna's tent and called, "Anna, do you want to go look for a Christmas tree?"

Anna came out of the tent, braiding her hair. "Where would we find a tree around here?"

"Well, maybe not a tree, but something. It just will not be Christmas Eve without some kind of tree."

"Sure," Anna replied, "maybe it will make me forget my stomach."

They walked together silently. It was cloudy, and the ocean looked gray. Then Mina saw it — the tree.

"Anna, there it is!" Mina ran over to a piece of drift-wood lying on the wet sand.

"That?" asked Anna.

"Sure." Mina held the gnarled branch upright. "If we find some decorations, it will be a *Tannenbaum.*"

Mina and Anna carried the branch back to camp. They chose a spot in the center of the camp, dug a hole and planted the branch. People began to come out of their tents to see what the girls were doing.

"What is that supposed to be?" asked a boy child, Martin.

"This is going to be our Christmas tree," Mina told him cheerily. "Do you have something to put on it for decoration?"

Martin turned and ran back into his tent. In a moment he came out again with a red ribbon.

"Oh, perfect!" Mina clapped her hands together. She tied the red ribbon in a bow on the very top of the branch.

Other people began bringing ornaments — beads, shells, ribbons, candles. The ribbons of all colors were

48

strung around its branches. At last it was a *Tannenbaum*.

"I am proud of you, Mina." Papa put his arm around her. "You are a real pioneer girl."

That evening the whole camp gathered around the tree. Mina and Anna lit the candles, which flickered but kept burning. Papa pulled his harmonica out of his pocket and began to play.

Oh *Tannenbaum*, oh *Tannenbaum*,
How lovely are thy branches.

Mina's throat got very tight, and tears streamed freely down her cheeks as she sang, blurring the candlelight on the tree. The branches were not lovely at all. When the song was ended Mina ran and buried her face on Papa's warm chest, and began to sob.

"Now, now," said Papa patting her back, "you must not cry on Christmas Eve. We still have presents to give."

It had grown dark. Papa, Mama, and Mina wished all a merry Christmas, and returned to their tent.

"I have a surprise for you, Mina." Papa reached under his blanket and pulled out something wrapped in a scarf. *"Fröhliche Weihnachten* my *kleine* Mina."

Mina unfolded the scarf carefully. And there in her hand was a little figure of a seagull with its wings spread in flight, carved from driftwood.

"Oh, Papa, it is beautiful." She held it up toward the sky and made it fly. Then Mina flung her arms around his neck and kissed his cheek. "Thank you, dear Papa."

Mama reached inside a box and brought out another package. *"Fröhliche Weihnachten,* Mina."* She handed Mina the soft package with a dark green ribbon tied around it. Mina untied the ribbon, opened up the package. There was a tiny red velvet cape — for Johanna — with tiny buttons to fasten it at the neck, and all lined with satin.

"How pretty, Mama! Johanna will look so fine." Mina kissed Mama's smooth cheek. "Thank you, Mama." Then Mina pulled Johanna out from her blankets, and fastened on the red cape. How elegant she looked.

Mina gave Papa and Mama the shells she had found. Mama said her shell was just the thing to hold her needle and thread. And Papa said, "Why it is shaped like a coin."

"Ja, and there is a Christmas star on it too. It will bring you good luck, I know, Papa."

They wished each other a Merry Christmas again, and then Papa blew out the candle.

Long after Papa and Mama were asleep, Mina lay awake. She thought about the Christmas feast last year — roast goose, baked apples, potatoes. It made her mouth water. Would tomorrow really be Christmas?

The wind had stopped blowing, and Mina crawled out of the tent very quietly so as not to awaken Papa and Mama. Outside the sky had cleared. All was quiet and still, as though the whole universe were holding its breath. And there, low on the horizon, was a single bright star. It was so big and bright that all the other stars looked dim beside it. The Christmas star, thought Mina, and kept gazing at it.

> Silent night, Holy night,
> All is calm, all is bright . . .

Those words had never had so much meaning as they did this night.

Suddenly the quiet was broken by a woman's cry. Mina looked around. Where had it come from? She felt her heart thumping hard inside her chest.

"Papa, Papa, wake up!"

"What is it, Mina? Where are you?"

"Out here."

Papa struggled out of the tent. "What happened?"

Just then the night was pierced by shrill baby's crying.

"*Frau* Kaufmann!" Mina said at once.

"But it is not her time yet." Mama was coming out of the tent. Yet the crying went on.

"The baby thinks it is time though, Mama."

"*Ja*, Mina. We must go and see if they need our help."

People were gathering at the Kaufmanns' tent, standing with coats over their night clothes. A light glowed from inside. Anna rushed over to the Jordans.

"Mina, Mina, I have a baby sister."

Mina thought of the star and of the baby. "Anna, it is just like the first Christmas. Look there." Mina pointed up at the star.

"So it is," Anna said with awe in her voice.

9

MAMA IS GONE

One cold wet morning in January a steamer anchored offshore. Mina watched from the tent as a smaller boat rowed toward the beach.

"Papa, look, the men are bringing lumber."

Papa looked out the door. "I hope they bring no more immigrants. Lumber we can use, but not more mouths to feed."

The little boat made several trips carrying lumber and some wooden crates. Then two men were left on shore, and the steamer weighed anchor.

People had gathered on the beach to talk to the men. Papa started out the tent, and Mina followed close behind.

"I will be back soon, Minchen."

Mama did not feel well, and had a fever. "Very well, Ernst."

When they reached the group, Mina heard one of the men say, "I am Joseph Reuss, a doctor," and he began shaking hands with those who stood nearby. He was a young, gentle looking man who wore eyeglasses and carried a black bag. "And this is my friend, Henry Huck. We are from New Orleans. We heard of your plight, and decided to come here to help."

Papa stepped up and shook hands with both men. "My name is Ernst Jordan, and we welcome you." Papa looked around at the group standing there. "Almost every one of us here has a loved one who is sick."

"So I have heard," said Doctor Reuss. "I will do my best for each and everyone." Then, holding up his bag for all to see, he added, "Here I have medicines that will help. And in these boxes we have brought food supplies." He turned to Huck, "My friend here has a lumber yard. He is donating this lumber to get some shelters built."

"We appreciate all this, of course," replied *Herr* Kaufmann. "But we are anxious to be off from this place to our land. In fact, some have left on foot."

"The *Verein* has failed us," Papa added. "There has been no sign of wagon teams. We have had to go hungry — our children are hungry. Have they forgotten us here?"

Doctor Reuss shook his head sadly. Looking at Papa he said, "In Galveston I learned that the creeks and rivers are up and impossible to cross. But Baron von Meusebach, the Verein's new leader, has promised that as soon as the rivers are down, he will get wagon teams through to you."

This news brought cheers and shouts from the group gathered around the doctor. "It is about time. Thank God!"

Doctor Reuss began to unpack the food supplies. There was salt cured ham, ship's biscuits, potatoes, and dried fruit.

53

People crowded around him, pushing to get a share of the food before it was all gone. Mina felt herself being jostled, but she fought back, using her elbows, to stay by Papa. He took one of her hands in his.

"Stop shoving!" shouted Doctor Reuss. "There will be enough for all . . . Now, form a line over here, and I will give a portion to the head of each family." As Doctor Reuss handed out slices of ham and other supplies he warned, "Make it last as long as possible."

When Papa and Mina returned with the supplies, Mama seemed cheered. Papa made a small fire with driftwood and bush limbs they had gathered. Mama cut off a piece of the ham and boiled it with a ship's biscuit to thicken the soup. It was too salty, but it was warm, and Mina felt nourished.

Day after day the men of the camp worked building a shelter. Doctor Reuss was kept busy nursing the sick, going from tent to tent in the cold rain.

Mama had begun to cough more and more. Her face had grown pale, and she had little appetite. Although Mama shivered under the blankets, her forehead felt very hot to Mina.

"I am afraid it is pneumonia," Mina heard Doctor Reuss say to Papa outside the tent. "There are many cases."

Mina knew that three people of the camp had died from pneumonia. The very word made her heart leap. But not Mama. It could not happen to Mama, Mina thought.

When Doctor Reuss had left, Mina asked Papa, "Will Mama get well?"

Papa's eyes were sad as he looked down at her, and

patted her shoulders. "We must do everything Doctor Reuss said, and be sure she takes the medicine."

Everyday Mina went over to the little wooden house some distance from the camp. It was the only house anywhere about. Mrs. White made a pot of broth every morning to give to the sick.

Mina took a small tin pail with her. She knocked at the door. Mrs. White could not speak much German, but she had a kind face and smiled at Mina as she poured some steaming broth into the pail.

Mama was too weak to sit up and eat the broth. Mina had to feed her tiny spoonfuls at a time.

"You are a good nurse, Mina."

"I want you to get well soon, Mama. Doctor Reuss said this broth would give you strength."

Mama sighed. "Enough now, Mina."

"But, Mama, try to take a little more."

"I cannot," Mama turned her face away.

Mina let Mama's head gently back down on the pillow. Mama seemed to be slipping away from her.

"Mina," Mama started and then paused.

"*Ja?*"

"Mina . . . you are so young. I do not know how to say this."

"What is it, Mama?" Mina felt uneasy about whatever Mama wanted to say.

"If I . . . if I should go . . ."

"No, Mama do not say that."

"I must, Mina . . . no, listen to me and do not interrupt."

Mina's throat felt tight.

"If I go, do not weep long." Mama reached over and

held Mina's hand. "Papa will need you to be strong."
Then Mama began to cough and cough.

Mina got out the medicine, and gave her a spoonful.
The coughing had worn her out. As soon as the spell was
over she fell peacefully to sleep. Mina sat watching her.
The blankets rose and fell as Mama breathed.

Mina closed her eyes and bowed her head. "Dear
God, please make Mama well."

But Mama did not get well. She grew weaker and
weaker. No longer did she take the broth Mina brought.

So many people in the camp were sick that Doctor
Reuss hardly had time to sleep. Even with his treatment
many died. Mina knew this. Papa and the other men had
used lumber to build caskets instead of shelter. And
Mina had heard the crying. Had God forsaken them on
this lonely beach?

One night when Papa and Mina were preparing for
bed, Mama said, "Ernst, call Doctor Reuss."

Papa looked at Mina, and without a word she ran
over to the doctor's tent.

"Doctor Reuss, you must come right away."

"*Ja*, I am coming."

When they entered the tent, Papa was leaning over
Mama. She was saying something to him so softly.

"Ernst, you must take Mina away from here," Mama
whispered.

"I will, Minchen, and you also as soon as you are
well."

The doctor knelt beside Mama to examine her. He
took her pulse. Then he took a bottle from his bag, and
gave Mama a spoonful. He looked at Papa in such a way
that Mina knew there was no hope. Papa and Doctor

Reuss went outside while Mina stayed by Mama holding her hand.

When Papa came back into the tent his eyes were wet. "Minchen, do not worry. I promise to find a wagon for us to leave this place."

Mama seemed to relax and smiled weakly at Papa and then at Mina. Papa leaned down and kissed Mama's cheek. She closed her eyes, and just stopped breathing.

Mina saw that Mama was not breathing. "Papa, Papa! Do not let her die. Do something!" Mina shook her hands helplessly.

Papa was looking at Mama's face, so pale in the candlelight. He reached over and held her face with his hand. "Oh, Minchen, why did I bring you to this dreadful place?" He laid his head on Mama's breast, and wrapped his arms around her. "Oh, Minchen, Minchen."

Mina put her head down on Papa's back, and held on for dear life. "Mama is gone, Mama is gone," she sobbed, over and over.

Mina thought back to that night in Wehrstedt when she lay awake dreaming of Texas. But instead of a dream, it was a nightmare. If only she could awaken and find that she was safe again in Opa's house.

Papa and Mina worked at building a casket for Mama. It was a sad job, but having work to do helped Mina. She held the lumber while Papa sawed. Then she helped him fit each piece into place. Papa did not talk much, and they worked silently.

Mina could not believe that Mama was really gone. Maybe she would wake up and call her. But Mama did not awaken. Mina tried not to think about putting Mama in this box and then underground.

"Papa, where is Mama now?" Mina asked. Papa stopped working and looked at Mina. "Do you think she might fly with the seagulls up to heaven?"

"Perhaps so, my *kleine* Mina, perhaps so."

"Do you remember what she said once, Papa?"

"What, Mina?"

"She said she wished she could fly like the gulls, right up to the heavens."

"*Ja*, I remember." Papa nodded his head.

At twilight *Herr* Kaufmann, *Herr* Hessler, and four other men carried Mama's casket along the beach. Papa, Mina, and friends followed along behind. Papa was holding Mina's hand as they walked. In her other hand Mina clutched the little wooden seagull Papa had made for her. The wind was blowing from the north as they walked up from the beach to the burial site.

The men lowered the casket into the ground. Papa held Mina tightly. Then Mina pulled the seagull out of her pocket, broke away from Papa, and laid it on top of Mama's casket.

"Fly away, Mama, fly away from here." Then Mina ran back to Papa, and hid her face against his chest. She did not want to see Mama's casket covered with earth. In her mind's eye she saw her little gull fly away from the casket.

"Goodbye, Mama," Mina cried. And she clutched Papa around the waist.

Papa led Mina away, back toward the beach.

Mina looked up toward the heavens. "Papa, maybe

Mama is watching us right now. And she is saying, 'Take care of Papa, Mina'.''

Papa tightened his grip on Mina's shoulder.

"I will, Mama," Mina said.

"And I will take care of our *kleine* Mina, Minchen." Papa looked upward. "We will survive, with God's help."

10

A WAGON AND OXEN

In March the rains stopped, and at last the land began to dry out. Still, no wagons came to take them inland to the German colony at New Braunfels.

Mina often thought of Mama and of her last words to Papa, "You must take Mina away from here." Papa's face looked so sad at times when he was quiet. Mina knew he was thinking about Mama.

Many people had left the beach on foot. But Papa thought that was unwise. "We will wait just a little longer."

"Papa, I cannot stand it here any longer. I would rather walk than stay on this gloomy beach watching people die one after another." The tightness came to Mina's throat as she thought of poor weak Mama lying on the damp tent floor.

"We will wait, Mina," Papa said with a finality she could not question.

One evening as the sun was disappearing below the flat horizon, Mina heard a rumbling noise. Far in the distance beyond the pond and across the treeless prairie a lone covered wagon pulled by two yokes of oxen came slowly toward the beach. As it came closer Mina saw that two people walked alongside, and the others rode.

Mina ran to meet the wagon, across the hard sand beach and through the clumps of grass. She waved at them as she ran, her braids flying. A man walking beside the wagon waved back, but he looked very tired. A boy walked beside him. There was a woman with two small children in the wagon. Mina stopped breathlessly as she came up.

"Where are you going?" Mina asked breathing heavily, and matching her step to theirs.

"Back to Germany, I hope, my child," the man replied. His mouth formed a smile, but his eyes remained sad.

Mina was suddenly aware that here was their long-awaited wagon, and her heart began to pound.

"Then you will not be needing the wagon anymore?"

"Well, I doubt that we could get very far across the ocean in it!" Again the smile came, and his somber face brightened a little.

"Then we would like to buy it from you, and the oxen too," Mina blurted out as she walked alongside with the man. "My Papa has some money. He did not give it all to the *Verein.*"

The man turned to look at his wife. Her eyes seemed sunken, and her cheeks wrinkled before her time. She shook her head to say no.

"We need all the money we can get for the wagon and oxen to buy our passage back to Germany," he told Mina.

By this time they were nearing the camp, and a crowd of people had gathered.

"I must sell to the highest bidder," the man said.

All Mina could think of was that Papa must get the wagon and oxen. In fact, it seemed their very lives depended upon this wagon. So many people were getting sick. Mina was no longer shocked when a death occurred. It happened every day. Who would be next? What if Papa ... Mina shuddered at the thought of being left alone.

On the beach people crowded around and completely surrounded the newcomers, talking all at the same time.

"Will you sell the wagon and oxen?" someone shouted.

The crowd pushed closer, and people struggled to get next to the wagon.

"What will you take for your wagon and oxen?" asked another.

Mina was getting pushed and shoved. Suddenly she went down on her hands and knees and escaped under the wagon where she felt safe as she listened to the shouts, and was surrounded by the feet of the crowd. The man stepped up on a spoke and into the wagon, and then Mina heard his voice above the noise.

"What am I bid? I must have enough for passage back to Germany."

"Seventy-five dollars," came a voice. The crowd quieted.

"Eighty dollars," she heard Papa say.

The bidding continued among the few who had money in their pockets.

"Eighty-five," came from *Herr* Kaufmann.

Suddenly Mina had an idea. Papa and *Herr* Kaufmann could buy the wagon together. She looked out from under the wagon. She could see nothing but a forest of legs, but she knew where Papa was standing. Mina crawled out, and pushed her way through to him.

"Papa!" she motioned for him to put his head down close, and she whispered her idea to him. "And we could take turns riding and walking," she finished.

"*Ja*, you are right, Mina." Then he whispered in her ear. "Run and tell *Herr* Kaufmann. Tell him I can bid ninety dollars."

Mina's heart was pounding. If they missed this chance to get a wagon, there might not be another.

"I will give you one hundred dollars," someone shouted.

Mina's heart leaped.

"*Herr* Kaufmann is on the other side," Papa whispered. "Hurry, Mina."

Mina began making her way through the crowd. She felt glad she was small for her age, and could slip between people without much notice. Even so, sometimes she had to push hard to get through the crowd, and people gave her ugly looks. But she had only one thought in her mind: Get to *Herr* Kaufmann. On the other side of the wagon she saw him.

"*Herr* Kaufmann!" Mina motioned for him to lean down, and she whispered to him.

Someone bid one hundred and twenty-five dollars.

Herr Kaufmann straightened, his eyes excited, held up his arm and said, "I bid one hundred fifty dollars." The crowd became hushed. There were no more bids.

"Sold then," said the wagon owner.

The crowd began to move apart. Papa made his way over to them.

"Oh, Papa, at last we have our wagon." Mina threw her arms around him.

"*Ja*, thanks to you, my *kleine* Mina." Then Papa shook hands with *Herr* Kaufmann, and they all drew closer to the wagon where the man was unhitching the oxen.

"My name is Ernst Jordan." Papa reached out his hand to shake. "And this is Heinrich Kaufmann, my new partner." Papa chuckled.

"I am Wilhelm Lange," answered the man as they all shook hands, "and my wife and children." His son looked down at his shoes, and dug in the sand with his heel.

"Well, I hope that a coastal steamer will come soon from Galveston," Papa said.

"*Ja*, we have had enough of Texas." *Herr* Lange looked at the ground and shook his head. "I hope you find better luck."

"Thank you, we shall try."

Herr Lange looked up at Papa. "Have you heard that Texas has joined the United States?"

"No, but it does not surprise me greatly."

"And the United States Army is hiring all teamsters to use their wagons for hauling supplies," *Herr* Lange added. "It appears there will soon be war with Mexico."

"Well, we go on with our private war."

Then Papa and *Herr* Kaufmann took out their money, counted it, and gave it to the man.

"That is one hundred fifty dollars," said Papa.

"Many thanks."

Before dawn Mina and Papa knelt beside Mama's grave.

"Minchen, we come to say our last farewell," Papa began and then paused. He seemed unable to go on, and he tightened his grip on Mina's shoulder. Then drawing

64

a deep breath he continued, "If only you were by my side once more . . . but I know you are happy to see us leave."

Mina looked up at the sky. "*Auf Wiedersehen,* Mama." She imagined the little seagull flying above as she and Papa knelt silently for a moment longer. Then the tip of the orange sun ball appeared at the edge of the sea. As it rose the first rays of sunlight shone upon them. It was time to leave this beach forever.

11

BETTER DAYS WILL COME

The Kaufmanns were waiting by the wagon when Mina and Papa returned.

"Now, Eva," Papa said to *Frau* Kaufmann, "you and the baby will ride, and we will walk. I think the girls may take turns riding if they get tired. Is that agreeable with you?"

"Very well, Ernst." She climbed into the wagon holding the baby.

Papa stood beside the oxen holding onto the yoke. "All right, get up," Papa slapped one of the oxen on the rump.

The wagon creaked as the big wheels began to turn. Papa carried his shotgun over his shoulder, and walked with *Herr* Kaufmann. Mina and Anna took hands, and began to skip along beside the plodding oxen, swinging their arms and singing, "New Braunfels we are com-ing, New Braunfels we are com-ing."

Then Mina turned to Papa. "Papa why is it that we go to New Braunfels instead of our land?"

"Well, Mina, we do not know where our land is or whether we even have any land. So, we must go to New Braunfels where the *Verein* has its headquarters. There we will find out what to do, and I will give the Commissioner General a piece of my mind for allowing his countrymen to be stranded on the beach."

"Papa, do you think Anna and I will be neighbors?"

Papa chuckled. "That we shall have to wait and see."

Miles and miles of flat grassy prairie spread out before them without a tree in sight. The sea, the miserable beach and tents were behind. Here and there were low marshy ponds like silver mirrors in the grass. Long legged white birds were standing in the shallow waters fishing with their beaks. As the wagon approached the birds unfolded their wings, and rose sharply in flight, legs dangling below them.

They walked all day long. Mina was too tired to skip and dance anymore. Anna was riding in the wagon with her mother. Mina looked down at her feet. They felt very sore on the bottoms, and her right shoe was rubbing her little toe. "You just keep on going," she commanded them to herself, "left, right, left, right."

In the late afternoon they saw the first trees on the horizon — like giant bushes.

"That must be Chocolate Creek," Papa said, "that *Herr* Lange talked about."

"*Ja*, it will be a good camping site for tonight," *Herr* Kaufmann suggested.

As they came to the small creek at last, Mina saw that the water was muddy.

"Now I know why it is called Chocolate Creek. Look at the water!"

Anna wrinkled her nose and stuck out her tongue.

"Mmm," Mina licked her lips and rubbed her stomach. "We can heat it up and have hot chocolate for supper. How delicious!"

The grassy winding bank looked like a cozy place to sleep, protected from the wind and sheltered by the giant spreading trees.

"Come, Anna, let us gather some wood for a fire." Mina began to fill her skirt with twigs.

Papa was loading his gun as *Herr* Kaufmann unhitched the oxen to let them graze.

"I will try to get us a prairie chicken for supper. You girls keep in that direction." Papa pointed downstream. "And do not make noise."

"*Ja*, Papa."

The sun was low and making silhouettes of the tree branches when they got the campfire started, using the flint. Then a shot rang out. Somehow Mina knew that Papa's hunt had been successful. Before long she heard the swish, swish of Papa walking through the grass. When he strode into the light of the campfire he was holding a plump prairie chicken by the neck. He smiled broadly as he stood there so erect, feet apart, the chicken held proudly at arm's length.

"How do you manage to be such a good hunter?" *Herr* Kaufmann asked.

"Well, I tell you, Heinrich, when it is necessary, one learns to do what one has never done before."

That night Mina went to sleep on the soft grass. Her hunger was satisfied. But as the fire died down she began to feel the loneliness of the prairie creep in. It was very dark; no moon was out. Papa covered the coals to keep them hot for morning. Darkness spread all about, and it seemed to Mina that they were the only people on earth. It was frightening to be on the cold, dark side of the earth in the middle of a wilderness.

Mina was awakened early by doves cooing to one another. It was a lovely sad sound, and she lay there in her blanket listening as daylight returned. Papa and *Herr* Kaufmann had a fire going. *Frau* Kaufmann was tending the baby who had begun to fret and cry.

"Anna, are you awake?" asked Mina. The bundled form next to her began to move like a giant caterpillar about to emerge as a butterfly.

"*Ja*, Mina."

Papa had made coffee which they drank with some ship's biscuits that Doctor Reuss had brought.

"We must move on to Victoria," Papa said. "*Herr* Lange told me we could purchase some supplies there for the rest of our journey."

It would take two more days to reach Victoria. Mina's legs moved automatically now, without her will— left, right, and carried her along. The baby began to cry more and sleep less.

"I am afraid she has a fever, Heinrich," said *Frau* Kaufmann. "Her forehead is hot."

The day had turned cloudy — low rippled clouds, and

the wind was chilling. Baby Elizabeth's crying chilled Mina too. Even the oxen seemed saddened by the crying, and their heads hung low under the weight of the yoke. If only we could get to Victoria, Mina thought.

"Papa, do you think there will be a doctor in Victoria?"

"I hope so, Mina." Papa did not look at her as she walked beside him. He looked straight ahead, not allowing Mina to know his thoughts. His wide mouth was grimly set.

But that night the baby cried and cried. No one slept. Mina lay with her eyes open, seeing nothing. The tiny shallow cry became weaker and weaker. And then with a gasp, it stopped altogether.

The momentary stillness was broken by *Frau* Kaufmann's anguished cry, "My baby, oh God, my baby. She has stopped breathing."

Mina put her hands over her ears. She did not want to hear. When she took them away, she heard *Frau* Kaufmann crying while *Herr* Kaufmann repeated over and over, "Why, why did I bring you to this terrible land?"

Why, indeed? wondered Mina. It had seemed like a great adventure to her once, but now . . .

Mina did not know she fell asleep, but suddenly it was dawn. She had that heavy feeling — after falling asleep sad. *Frau* Kaufmann was weeping as she wrapped little Elizabeth in a blanket. They buried her beneath the feathery bush tree where they had camped. Papa found a flat stone and scratched the letters E M K with the point of his knife and placed it at the head of the grave.

They bowed their heads. Mina put her arm around Anna's shoulders as *Herr* Kaufmann spoke a prayer.

Father, we leave a part of ourselves,
Our beloved Elizabeth,
Here under the boughs of this tree.
Show us the way,
Give us the strength
To go on . . .

Amen.

Herr Kaufmann led his wife to the wagon, his arm around her. Her face was hidden in her hands.

They walked or rode silently that day, and took turns riding beside poor *Frau* Kaufmann who was, in turn, weeping quietly as the wagon bumped along, or looking grimly ahead.

Beside the road they began to see abandoned possessions scattered along the way — bundles of clothing, cooking pots and utensils, a tattered blanket. Then a little distance off the road Mina saw the mound of a grave, and then another. At the sight of the graves *Frau* Kaufmann began to sob again. *Herr* Kaufmann, sitting beside her, had tears in his eyes as his wife laid her head on his shoulder.

Mina felt cold inside. Death was becoming their constant companion, and she could feel it hovering over them, threatening.

"Papa, are those graves of people who left Indian Point earlier?" She already knew the answer. Papa put his arm around her as they walked sadly along.

"Mina, you and I are strong. We will survive this trial. We will endure." Papa straightened his shoulders and seemed to become taller. "And then, better days will come, remember that, better days will come."

"I will, Papa." Tears rolled down Mina's cheeks. She

wiped them off with the back of her hand as they walked along silently. She squared her shoulders and tilted up her chin. The creak of the wagon was the only sound.

12

IN GOOD HANDS

By late afternoon they were coming closer and closer to the Guadalupe River on the left and the thick clumps of trees that followed its edges. Nearby the river lay the town of Victoria with its scattered houses. It was the first town Mina had seen since Galveston. Smoke rose from the chimneys in the distance, and made her feel safe again. She forgot her tired legs and sore feet, and caught Papa's hand, skipping along.

"Oh, Papa, I wish we could stay here to live." She looked up at him for an answer.

"Well, Mina, we have no land here." Papa patted her hand. "We must go on to New Braunfels. It is a good town, I hear, you will see."

Houses stood here and there along the road into Victoria. Some were log buildings, some were made of boards, and others were adobe. The center of town was an empty grassy square where trees had been newly planted.

People moved about the town, and stopped to watch as the Jordans and Kaufmanns came slowly to the square. Once again Mina heard English spoken, but also she heard Spanish. And she saw, for the first time in her life, some negro slaves. There was a little negro boy running along beside his mother holding onto her skirts with one hand. His mother carried a basket on her head, holding it in place with one hand. She looked very proud and exotic.

"Ho!" called Papa, and stopped the wagon in front of a log house on the square.

A man stood on the long front porch. His wife was in the doorway with a child on each side.

"*Guten Abend,*" Papa said taking off his hat.

"*Guten Abend,*" the man returned his greeting.

"So, you are German also." Papa and *Herr* Kaufmann shook hands with the man and introduced themselves. The man's name was Hans Schumann, from the village of Himmelsthur.

"We came in the spring of 1840, and decided to stop here."

"Are you glad you left Germany?" Papa asked.

"Now I am glad," answered *Herr* Schumann. "At first it was hard, very hard work. But, you see, here in Texas it is different from Germany. There are no rich noblemen looking down their noses at farmers. No, here we are all equal, and we all work." The man surveyed his house, his garden, and with a sweep of his arm he said, "Now I am rewarded for my hard work with all this, and I am free to live here as I choose."

"I look forward to the time when we can make such a

74

home for ourselves," said Papa. "We are on our way to New Braunfels from Indian Point."

Herr Schumann nodded. "*Ja,* some have gone before you, and I am afraid some never made it this far. It must have been a terrible winter at Indian Point."

"Scarcely a family was spared the loss of a loved one. My own wife perished during the winter, and on the way here Heinrich's baby girl . . ." Papa paused, searching for words.

"It is too much," *Herr* Schumann shook his head sadly, "too much suffering."

"And hundreds of people are still stranded on the beach, dying everyday. Something must be done for them. The *Verein* must send wagons," Papa said.

Frau Schumann came out of the house bringing a pitcher of milk and two cups. She poured some into each cup, and handed one to Mina and one to Anna, smiling.

"I imagine you girls have not had any milk for awhile."

Mina took the cup. "Thank you very much." The milk was still warm and foamy. It tasted so creamy that Mina drank it down without stopping. Foam covered her upper lip and tickled.

Frau Schumann laughed heartily, and poured another cup. "You could use a little fat on your bones, my child. And you, too," she told Anna, pouring another cup for her. "Well now, it is getting late, and you will need a place to stay the night. You are welcome to sleep in our loft. The children can sleep downstairs tonight." *Frau* Schumann was a plump, pretty lady, and had a comforting smile. Mina already liked her.

"You are very kind, *Frau* Schumann," Papa said.

"And we accept your offer with pleasure," added

75

Herr Kaufmann. He took his wife by the arm, and they all walked to the house.

Frau Schumann took Mina's hand and Anna's. "Come then, we will have a little supper." Her hand felt warm and friendly as she led them into the house.

The two little boys had grown brave enough to come out on the porch where they watched everything with big eyes. The youngest had his thumb in his mouth.

Inside the house *Frau* Schumann lighted a candle, and set it on the table that stood before the hearth, where a small fire was glowing. Laid out upon the table were cheese, bread, and the pitcher of milk. *Frau* Schumann went to the cupboard, and took out a jar of jelly. Everything was so neat and clean that Mina knew they were in good hands. The floor of the cabin was made of wooden planks, and the log walls were stuccoed inside and whitewashed.

"Come, let us sit down to supper." *Herr* Schumann brought two more chairs, and they all sat at the table. It was so cozy and safe in the house. As *Herr* Schumann said the blessing, Mina wished they could stay here forever.

That night Mina, Papa, Anna, and her parents climbed the ladder on the wall up to the loft. They lay down on corn shuck mattresses, but it was the softest bed Mina had slept on since they left their home in Wehrstedt. Light glowed from downstairs through the square opening in the loft floor. Mina wondered if she and Papa would ever have a home like this.

The next morning as Mina and Papa and the Kaufmanns were leaving, *Frau* Schumann gave them some bread and cheese to take along. Mina felt rested by the night in the cozy loft. Her feet no longer hurt, and the sunlight was warm on her face.

"You have been so kind. Many thanks," said Papa to the Schumanns.

Mina flung her arms around *Frau* Schumann which surprised her. She laughed her hearty laugh and hugged Mina.

"Now, you can stop by Gramann's store on the other side of the square to get your provisions," *Frau* Schumann reminded them.

"Thank you," Papa said. *"Auf Wiedersehen,"*

"Auf Wiedersehen," everyone called.

"Good luck," called *Herr* Schumann.

13

NIGHT VISITOR

The road to New Braunfels was a long one. They walked and sometimes rode for days on end, always keeping within sight of the Guadalupe River. Some days it rained on them, and Mina shivered in her wet clothes.

Now there were more trees, and the land rolled up into low hills. In the valleys, forests of many kinds of trees grew, some with very broad leaves. And the open meadows were blanketed with wild flowers. They passed farm houses scattered along the way, and small towns — Cuero, then Gonzales.

One night in camp after everyone had lain down to sleep, Mina was awakened by something moving about in the branches of the big tree that spread out above. Anna lay sleeping beside her, and Mina touched her shoulder gently.

"Anna, are you awake?"

Whatever was up in the tree stirred. Mina's heart be-

gan to pound. The night was perfectly dark with no moon at all.

"Anna," Mina repeated.

Anna stirred sleepily. "What is it, Mina? What is the matter?"

"Do you hear something up in the tree?"

Both girls were silent, listening. There was no sound.

"No, Mina, I hear nothing."

Mina sat up on her blanket. She remembered her vision of an Indian with a raised tomahawk.

"What if it is an Indian?" Mina whispered.

Anna caught her breath. "Oh, Mina," was all she said.

Papa lay a few feet away, on the other side of the campfire. Mina knew he had his gun beside him, loaded.

There were still some glowing coals. Mina crawled over to the coals, and put some kindling on them. Soon a flame flared up, shining on the girls' faces. Anna looked paralyzed with fear, her eyes big, her mouth open, but saying nothing. Mina shielded her eyes from the firelight, and looked into the tree.

Papa stirred awake at the light. "Mina, what are you doing?" He grabbed his gun and jumped up.

"Papa, there is something up in the tree. I heard it moving about."

By this time the Kaufmanns had awakened.

"What is it, Ernst? What is happening?" *Herr* Kaufmann asked.

Then Mina saw it. She saw two eyes shining in the firelight, nothing more.

"Papa, there it is," she screamed, pointing to a thick branch that reached out directly above them.

"Stay down," warned Papa, and he took aim carefully at the eyes.

80

The gun went off and echoed through the valley. Then in the firelight a great cat leaped from the branch, and ran off into the darkness.

For a moment everyone was silent. The explosion of the gun still in her ears, Mina stood up. In that circle of light she felt small in the vastness of Texas.

"That was a panther!" said *Herr* Kaufmann, breathlessly.

"Well, he will not return tonight," Papa said, lowering his gun. "That panther was after our provisions. I am sure of it."

Mina wondered if that was all he was after.

The road continued on and on through the rolling hills. Almost three weeks had passed since they left the beach. Mina felt so weary. Had she been walking all her life? It seemed so. She was thinner, and the Texas sun had baked her skin brown and her hair even more golden.

In the north a dark bank of clouds moved in their direction. It made everything in the sunlight look even brighter. The air was still. Then the cloud spread over the sky, blotting out the sun, and a cold wind began to blow. Mina got her coat out of the wagon, and *Frau* Kaufmann wrapped a shawl around her shoulders.

"Well, we are in for a cold night." Papa held onto his hat as the wind whipped his coat. "But we should be getting to New Braunfels soon."

The road led closer and closer to a bend in the river. The town of New Braunfels came into sight on the opposite high bank. In spite of the cold wind Mina jumped up and down happily. She and Anna joined hands and danced about.

"We are here, we are here," Mina sang. Even the cold could not chill her spirits.

81

"Thanks be to God," Papa said, and he halted the oxen as they came to a grove of trees.

Big raindrops began to fall, faster and faster until the rain poured down. They all took shelter in the wagon.

When the rain stopped for a moment. Papa got out. "Before darkness falls, I am going to have a closer look at the river."

"I will go too." Mina followed behind him.

As they walked down the bank, they saw a ferry boat tied to the other bank. The river had become swollen with rain, and the current tugged at the little ferry, threatening to carry it away downstream. On the branch of a tree near the rushing river hung a horn.

"Papa, look, here is a horn for calling the ferryman." Mina put the horn to her mouth and blew hard. It made a blast of sound. Mina blew again, but no one answered the call.

It had grown quite dark by this time. As Mina and Papa started back up the bank, someone called from the opposite side.

"Halloo . . . halloo, there."

Papa answered, "Halloo."

"You will have to wait till morning," came the voice again. "The river is too swift to cross by night."

"Very well," Papa answered.

There was only a cold supper that night. Mina wrapped blankets around her, and shivered, huddled sitting up next to Papa in the wagon.

The wind howled and tore at the blankets. Could it be, Mina wondered, that the little village across the river was to be their home in Texas at last?

14

A BIRTHDAY GIFT

By morning the rain had stopped. Mina crawled out and went down to the river. Two men were preparing to loose the ferry. Holding on to the rope which stretched across the river, they guided it safely to shore.

Papa and *Herr* Kaufmann hitched up the wagon, and they rode across on the ferry. On the other side the oxen had to strain to pull the wagon up the bank. Mina and the Kaufmanns pushed the wagon from behind until they reached level ground.

There before them was the village of New Braunfels — wooden houses of different sizes were scattered about among the trees on a small flat plain. It had the raw, temporary look of an army encampment. Still, with smoke coming from the chimneys it was a comforting sight. In the distance were rolling cedar covered hills, and to the left, rising out of the plain, was one low hill with a log building perched atop, overlooking the village.

Papa and *Herr* Kaufmann paid the ferryman.

"Can you direct us to the *Verein* headquarters?" asked *Herr* Kaufmann.

"*Ja*, sure. You see that building on the hill? That is the *Sophienburg*."

"Ah, so." Papa looked in that direction and nodded his head.

"Thank you very much," said *Herr* Kaufmann.

"You will find the Commissioner General of the *Verein* there — Meusebach," the ferryman continued.

The streets were muddy and rutted, and the oxen had hard work to pull the wagon along. When they arrived at the foot of the *Sophienburg*, Papa and Mina walked up the hill, leaving the Kaufmanns to watch over the wagon and oxen. As they approached the long low cabin, a man came out the door and stood on the porch, his hands clasped behind his back. He looked to be about Papa's age, and he had red hair and a full red beard.

"Are you Baron von Meusebach?" Papa asked, walking toward the porch.

"*Ja*, but I have dropped the Baron. Here in Texas I am simply John O. Meusebach, at your service."

"Well, you are a little late to be of service," Papa said bitterly. "I am Ernst Jordan. I paid my money to the *Verein* to come to Texas, only to find hundreds of Germans stranded on the beach with no way to travel inland. They are dying every day."

Meusebach shook his head sadly. "*Ja*, it is a terrible situation. The rains, and now the government takes all the wagons." He looked up at Papa. "We need more money to buy our own wagons, and I am determined to get it."

"It will be too late for many, as it was for my wife."
Papa looked away. "The promises sounded so good back
in Germany . . . so we came, only to find those promises
were empty."

Mina had never seen Papa so angry. He was usually
such a patient man. Papa's eyes were fastened intently
on *Herr* Meusebach, and he stood proud and straight.

"*Herr* Jordan, I am working day and night to make
good those promises. There are problems, but the *Verein*
has good intentions.

"Very well, we are here to claim our land."

Herr Meusebach stepped down from the porch and
came closer to them.

"*Herr* Jordan, the land to which you are entitled is
still inhabited by Indians. Come, let us go inside and I
will show you a map."

Indians! thought Mina. Had they come so far only to
be turned back by Indians? Mina shivered.

In the middle of a long room stood a roughhewn
table, and upon it was a map.

"Our plan is to establish a string of colonies closer
and closer to the land grant, here." He circled the spot on
the map. "Here is New Braunfels . . . the next colony is
to be here." *Herr* Meusebach looked up at Papa's face.
"We have surveyed this spot, and divided it up into one-
acre town lots and ten-acre farming lots."

"That is far less than we were promised."

"*Ja*, that is true. But as soon as a treaty can be made
with the Comanches, you will get your land also. Now,
my advice to you, *Herr* Jordan, is to join the first group
of settlers going to this new colony, which will be called
Fredericksburg. Preparations are being made to leave by
the end of this month."

"Very well." Papa drew a deep breath.

"Until then, you may camp in a vacant cabin that stands just off the square." He pointed it out to Papa. Then he gave them a sack of corn and some venison. "Provisions are distributed here each day at ten o'clock when available."

The cabin had one door in the front and small openings for windows, but no glass in them. There was a chimney at one end. Inside it was dark and damp with only a dirt floor. But with a fire popping and sparking on the hearth, and blankets hung for privacy, it seemed cozy to Mina. *Frau* Kaufmann cooked in the fireplace, and Mina and Anna helped her. For a table they used one of the boxes brought from Germany, and placed logs around it for chairs.

That first evening they were surprised to hear singing in the street, and ran outside. There came a group of *Verein* soldiers marching along in their tall riding boots. They had swords buckled on and carried rifles over their shoulders. As they drew closer Mina could hear the words to their song:

> Through the ocean's waves,
> Cut off from the Fatherland
> And many a bond of love
> We have come hither.
> On spirited mounts we cross
> The hot prairies of Texas
> And shorten the way with song
> Which rings to this sound
> Hail, Germany; Germany hail!

"What a fine group of young men," said *Frau* Kaufmann. "I feel better already."

86

Every day Papa and *Herr* Kaufmann went to the Sophienburg. Sometimes they returned with fresh meat and corn, and sometimes they returned empty handed.

A neighbor offered the use of his hand mill for grinding the corn. It was attached to a tree beside his cabin, and Mina and Anna took turns grinding as the other poured kernels into the black iron hopper on top of the mill.

When there was no corn distributed, they gathered acorns to grind instead.

On April fifth Mina awoke in the dark cabin, wondering if there would be anything about today to make it special. It was her eleventh birthday. Papa was already building up the fire. Mina dressed quickly, and came to the fire to put on her shoes and stockings.

"Well, happy birthday, my *kleine* Mina."

"Thank you, Papa."

He looked at her with a sad smile on his face. "My little girl is growing up before my eyes."

"Papa, I think I will go out and gather acorns this morning for bread."

"Very well, Mina, but ask Anna to go with you. And do not wander far from the settlement. There are Indians in the hills."

Mina knew that was true, for sometimes at night they could see Indian fires dotting the hillside. Mina felt curious about those campfires, but at the same time her scalp prickled at the thought of the savage Indians gathered about, gnawing and tearing at their food like animals.

"All right, Papa."

Mina and Anna walked over to Comal Creek, and followed along its winding bank. Big oaks grew here, and the girls began to gather acorns. Mina made a pouch with her apron and walked along picking up acorns here and there. Not many were to be found, as most had already been picked up by others or eaten by animals. So they had to go farther and farther. The creek was so clear, and the sun so warm that they sat down on the bank to watch the little fish that darted about. Mina dipped her hands and took a drink of the cool water.

"We had better go back, Mina. It is getting late."

"You go on, Anna, I want to find some more acorns."

"No, your Papa said we should stay together."

They wandered on a little farther, coming closer and closer to the hills when Mina heard a sound like the hooting of an owl. Somehow it did not sound exactly right. Then another owl answered.

A pang of fear shot through Mina, though she did not know why. She stood still, hardly breathing. Her eyes searched the woods. She turned her head slowly and looked to her left, to the right. And then she saw him — the Indian. Her heart began pounding wildly.

He stood on a rocky rise near the creek, tall and sinewy with a red robe draped around his waist. His long black hair, partly encased in a silver tube, draped over one shoulder, and only a silver breastplate covered his chest. He held a lance at arm's length propped on the ground.

Mina dropped her apron, and the acorns scattered to the ground. Her hands flew to her mouth and stifled a scream.

Anna turned and ran, screaming over her shoulder, "Run, Mina, run for your life."

But Mina stood stock still, paralyzed at the sight. This was the Indian of her wildest thoughts. What would he do? Did he want her blond scalp to decorate his tipi? Mina could not move, could not run.

His dark eyes were strangely piercing, for the lashes and brows had been plucked out, and a stripe of blue paint blazed across his forehead and over his eyelids. He made a sound, a word, and took his long hank of black hair in his hand.

Mina caught her breath. What did he want?

Then the tall Indian laid down his spear before him, stepped over it and came toward Mina. Her heart beat wildly, out of control. He took one of her blond braids in his hand and looked at it closely. Mina held her breath. Was he going to scalp her? She jerked her braid out of his hand.

He stepped back and motioned with his arm for someone to come. There was a rustling in the bushes, and an Indian woman and girl appeared riding on a horse. The Indian said something to the girl. She slid off the horse and came to him. She had on a deerskin skirt and poncho that were fringed, and a blue and white beaded belt. She looked at Mina, her dark eyes curious, but friendly. Mina felt less afraid. Her heart slowed its wild beating. The girl was Mina's age, and they looked at each other eye to eye.

The man spoke a word to the girl, and she undid the belt, holding it in her outstretched hand toward Mina. Mina took the belt in one hand, and it glittered in the sunlight. The girl said some words Mina could not understand. Then she smiled. She touched her own hair, pointed at Mina's hair and back at herself. Her other hand was clenched over something, and she offered it to Mina. It was a piece of bone sharpened like a knife on one edge. The girl held a hank of her own hair, and pretended to cut off a piece with the bone. She pointed again to Mina's hair.

"You want a piece of my hair?" Mina asked. "You want to trade?"

The girl had a puzzled look on her face.

That is it, thought Mina. She only wants a lock of my hair. Mina laid the belt on the ground, and took the bone from the girl. Pulling one of her braids taut in front of her face, she sawed at the loose hair just above the ribbon. The bone was quite sharp, and quickly made the cut. She pulled her other braid around, and did the same. The two tufts of hair, each tied with ribbon, she held in the open palms of her hands toward the girl.

"Here," said Mina.

The girl took the two tufts of hair, turned them about before her eyes, stroked them. She looked at Mina, smiled, and turned to her father, handing him the blond locks. He examined them carefully.

The Indian girl knelt and began to pick up the acorns which Mina had spilled, offering them in her outstretched palms to Mina, smiling. Mina was no longer frightened. She made a pouch of her apron, and together she and the Indian girl picked up all the acorns. Then Mina put the blue beaded belt on top.

Pointing to herself, the Indian girl said, "A-ma-ya."

Mina touched herself with her forefinger and spoke her name, "Mi-na," slowly. The girls looked at each other silently for a moment.

"Goodbye, Amaya." Mina took one last look at the Indian family. She turned and began to run toward home, clutching her apron in one hand. She stopped to look back once, and waved. The Indians stood just as she had left them, watching her. Mina turned and ran on toward the cabin.

90

"Papa, Papa," Mina called as she saw him up ahead, running toward her. Anna and her parents were right behind.

"Mina!" Papa held out one arm for her to fly into. In the other he carried the shotgun.

"Papa, oh Papa," but Mina was so out of breath she could hardly continue. "Indians!" She pulled the blue beaded belt out of her apron for all to see. "Look, Papa, a present for my birthday from the Indians."

15

ON TO FREDERICKSBURG

Mina looked ahead at the long line of wagons bumping along the rocky road. They were following an Indian trail through the hilly countryside.

"Papa, Texas is beginning to look like Germany."

"You are right, Mina."

"Remember what we said when we left Wehrstedt?"

"*Ja.*" Papa nodded his head thoughtfully.

"Well, I think my wish came true. We *are* going to live in the hills again." Mina flipped her braid over her shoulder. "How much longer till we get there?"

"Not long. We should see the Pedernales River late today."

"Will this be our home to stay forever?" Mina asked, and watched Papa's face as he answered.

"*Ja*, Mina, I think so."

Mina heaved a deep sigh. She hoped Papa really meant that, for she did not want to travel any farther.

The days had been long since they left New Braunfels.

The only exciting incident so far was when an old Indian had visited their camp one evening, and cured a man's infected foot by applying some kind of leaf to the wound. By the next day the swelling had gone down and the redness had disappeared. Mina wondered whether the healing was because of the leaf, or the magic words the old Indian had muttered while he pressed the leaf to the wound.

Now they were traveling more and more into Indian territory. Mina felt safe though with the *Verein* soldiers that were escorting the wagon train to the new colony. One of them rode by on his horse toward the head of the train. He looked so brave and handsome.

The day passed slowly. Mina was tired of games she and Anna had made up along the way. No one had spoken for a long while. Mina held a stick in one hand, and watched idly as the spokes of the wheel tapped it.

"Look, there is the river up ahead," Papa said.

The lead wagon halted, and everyone stopped. A soldier rode by swiftly, pulling his rifle from his shoulder.

"What is it, Papa?" Mina shielded her eyes from the sun in order to see better. On the riverbank just off the road was an Indian camp of tipis.

"Papa, Indians!" Mina pointed toward the camp.

The lead wagon started up again, and began to cross the river. A gunshot rang out.

"Behind the wagon, everyone," Papa commanded.

Mina stepped up on the wheel enough to see over the wagon. The whole wagon train had halted. *Herr* Kaufmann steadied the oxen as Papa made his gun ready.

"Are we being attacked, Heinrich?" asked *Frau* Kaufmann in a shrill whisper.

"Oh, Mama, are they going to scalp us?" Anna asked. Her eyes were wild with fear. *Frau* Kaufmann put her arm around Anna's shoulders.

Seeing Anna in such a fright made Mina feel determined to be brave — to look at what was happening with clear eyes. She felt the beaded belt around her waist and thought of Amaya.

At the river's edge Mina could see a group of men, soldiers and Indians, gathered around something on the ground. Their horses stood nearby. The men were gesturing to each other. The blade of a knife flashed in the sunlight as a soldier took it out of his belt.

Mina climbed down and stood beside Papa. He did not even notice as she moved away, up the wagon train, keeping behind the wagons as she went. Everyone was watching the group. No one noticed Mina. She reached the lead wagon, and stood on tiptoe to look over the backs of the oxen toward the group of men. They stood in a circle on the riverbank. Mina moved from behind the oxen to get a better look. At their feet lay the body of a black bear. An arrow protruded from his shoulder, and blood dampened his fur.

One of the Indians towered above the others, and in his long braid which rested over the front of his shoulder was blond hair! Mina caught her breath and covered her mouth with her hands. Was it possible that this was the same Indian? As her heartbeat quickened, she looked at him closely. Yes . . . he was the same. Mina's hand went up to her braid, and she felt the cut end absently. Just then she heard the Indian speak, and he pointed at her. All the men turned and looked at Mina. One of them motioned for her to come over.

"Well, little *Fräulein*," said the soldier, "it appears

that you are acquainted with Chief Custaleta." He pointed toward the tall Indian.

Mina looked once again into the exotic face that had so frightened her before. A chief, she thought. What a strange land this is. To think that I, a simple German girl, am friend to an Indian chief! Something stirred inside her as she looked at Custaleta. It was not fear, but a feeling there was a bond between them that no one else understood.

Then the silence was broken as the chief uttered some words, pointing first at the bear, then at the soldiers. Then he held out his hands in front of him, one clasped over the other.

"That means peace," said a soldier.

The chief spoke to the others. They mounted their horses, turned, and rode away toward the camp. As Chief Custaleta rode, the long braid with Mina's hair in it dangled gracefully behind. He turned once and looked at Mina.

"Well, I never saw anything like that," said the soldier. People began gathering around. "The Indians were arguing about who was going to have this bear I shot. Then a little girl comes up, and the chief backs down, just like that." He shook his head in disbelief.

Mina just stood there watching the Indians gallop back toward their camp. Then she heard the soldier talking to her.

"*Fräulein*, how do you know him?"

At first Mina could not speak. She turned and looked at the soldier, but she was thinking of the tall Indian. Then she took her braid in her hand again, and showed it to the soldier.

"Because . . . because I once gave him locks of my hair."

Suddenly Mina thought of Papa, turned and ran back to the wagon. Papa had started toward them.

"Papa, that was my Indian friend, and everything is all right. He is the chief!"

"Mina, why did you leave the wagon without telling me?" Papa held her at arm's length and looked at her closely.

"But Papa, I . . ."

Herr Kaufmann came up. "What was the shot?"

"It was only one of our soldiers shooting a bear." Mina said, "but the Indians had shot him too with an arrow."

Papa looked at Mina for a moment sternly, and then his face broke into a smile. He shook his head from side to side.

"You are quite a pioneer girl, Mina."

"Do you think we shall eat bear meat tonight, Papa?"

"*Ja*, Mina, the soldiers are butchering it now."

Would cousin Christine believe that she was eating bear meat in the wilderness, Mina wondered?

They got back into the wagon. Mina felt proud when she saw how Anna looked at her. The wagon train started up once more, and slowly they approached the river. Water came up to the axles, but it was flowing gently. The oxen held their heads up, and their eyes looked wild. But they trudged along obediently through the wide river, up the bank, and on the few more miles to the site of Fredericksburg.

The only sign that man had been here was a clearing and an unfinished blockhouse the surveyors had started. It was to be used for storing *Verein* supplies. The trees grew tall and the underbrush so thick that the clearing was the only place to make camp.

That night a huge fire blazed up in the center of the clearing, and the bear meat was roasted, fat side up. The firelight flickered on the wagons and surrounding forest, making the clearing an island of light and warmth.

16

THE CABIN

Mina had never seen Papa do such hard work. The sweat glistened on his arms and face, and his shirt was soaking wet as he swung his axe to cut a tree. When it fell at last, Papa straightened up, wiped his forehead on the back of his sleeve, and smiled at Mina. He looked happy to be doing this work. Mina helped by using the hatchet to chop off the smaller branches as Papa hacked away the larger ones. Then Papa wrapped a chain around the log, and hitched it up to the yoke of oxen. Together they walked beside the oxen as the log was dragged slowly back to their cabin site.

Papa had never built a house, but as he always said, "When it is necessary, one learns to do what one has never done before."

When the logs were all cut, neighbors came to help raise the walls. Mina liked having so many people around, working together. Anna came with her father. One of Mina's jobs was to bring drinking water from the creek. She and Anna struggled up the bank with the heavy wooden bucket, and set it down in the shade of a tree. Then everyone gathered around for a drink. When it was Papa's turn, he poured his first dipperful over his head. Everyone laughed.

"Now Ernst knows how to keep cool," *Herr* Kaufmann said.

Papa laughed heartily as the water dripped from his hair and beard.

Then *Herr* Kaufmann took the dipper and poured water over himself and some more over *Herr* Hessler, who grabbed the dipper and bucket, and began throwing dippers of water this way and that until everyone was wet and laughing. Finally he poured the remaining water over himself from the bucket.

Mina had never seen men, certainly not Papa, act so foolish. She and Anna stood watching. It seemed that something had broken loose inside all of them. For that brief moment they were a bunch of schoolboys at their pranks again. It was the first time Papa had really laughed since they came to Texas.

But there was work to be done — logs to be cut to length and notched — and the men became themselves again, and got to it. Mina held a log steady on the ground as Papa notched it on either end with his axe. Every time his axe hit, she felt the jolt through her whole body.

Then the men rolled the log into position, and strained together to lift and lay it in place. The walls went up slowly. By the next day, they got too high to reach. Papa leaned two logs against the house at an angle. Then ropes were tied to either end of a log, and it was hauled up.

The side walls went up into the gables. Everyone cheered as the ridgepole was laid in place from one gable

to the other. The top of the cabin had been reached! Then log rafters were hauled up and set, and long cedar shingles were nailed to them.

When the heavy work was done, Mina and Papa did the finishing by themselves. Papa made up lime mortar, and they both worked at chinking the cracks between the logs with rocks and mortar. Then Mina brought stones for Papa to line the fireplace.

Finally the last crack had been chinked, and Mina thought about the clock Opa had given them so long ago.

"We must unpack the clock, Papa."

Mina went inside the tent and found the clock at the bottom of a box, carefully wrapped in a blanket. She wound the clock, and placed it on the rough split log above the fireplace. It began to tick away the minutes, and life in their new home had started.

Fredericksburg began to look like a village. Clearings were made, cabins were started and finished, others started. More wagon trains came from New Braunfels, and the colony grew.

One day after the summer heat had come, Papa and Mina were sitting on the bench outside the cabin.

"Mina, I have been thinking that we need some money to buy a milk cow."

"Oh, I would like that, Papa, but where will we get the money?"

"Well, I have a plan." Papa puffed on his pipe. "The *Verein* needs wagons to haul supplies from New Braunfels. So Heinrich has agreed to sell the wagon and oxen to me, and I will work as a teamster for the *Verein*. What do you think of that, Mina? It means I would be away for weeks at a time. And you would have to stay with the Kaufmanns."

The thought of Papa leaving sent a pang of fear through Mina. What if something should happen and he never came back?

"Could I go with you, Papa?" Mina asked suddenly.

"Now Mina, you know our garden would go to weeds. And *Herr* Leyendecker will be starting his school soon. No, you must stay and take care of things."

The next days passed too quickly for Mina. She wished she could hold them back and keep Papa from going away. On the day Papa was to leave, Mina got up very early and cooked bacon and cornbread for him, while Papa hitched the oxen, and cleaned his shotgun. Then the time came for leaving.

"Come, Mina, I will take you to the Kaufmanns' cabin as I leave."

But Mina had some cleaning up to do, and besides, she did not want Anna to see her crying after Papa left.

"No, Papa, I will go over as soon as I finish here. Do not worry about me." Mina tried to smile cheerily at Papa as they stood beside the wagon.

"Very well, then, I will take my leave."

Mina's throat felt tight, and she struggled to keep the tears back.

"Now take care of yourself . . . and hurry back." Mina flung her arms around Papa, and he held her in his strong arms for a moment. She could not say anymore, or the dam inside her would surely break.

Then Papa held her at arm's length. "Remember, you are my pioneer girl."

Mina liked that. She looked up at Papa, smiled back at him, and nodded. "I know, Papa."

Papa climbed in the wagon, called "Get up" at the oxen, and the wagon started off slowly out to the road. Mina watched as Papa grew smaller. She heard him call "Haw" at the oxen to make them go left on the road. As they turned Papa waved.

"I will be back soon, Mina."

"*Auf Wiedersehen*, Papa." Mina wanted to run after the wagon, and go with Papa, but she did not move. She watched as Papa turned into the road and then was gone.

17

WHILE PAPA IS AWAY

When *Frau* Kaufmann took sick, Mina was sent to live with the Bickenbachs. The Kaufmanns were almost like her own family, and Mina wished she did not have to leave.

As she walked down the road to the Bickenbachs' that afternoon, she stepped up on every tree stump she came to. It was a game, and Mina could not pass one without first standing on top. The walk to the Bickenbachs' cabin took twice as long this way.

There was no one her age in the Bickenbach family. The children, two sons and two daughters, were all grown up, and only the daughters remained at home. When Mina came to their place on Austin Street, Lisette, the eldest daughter, stood in the doorway.

"Welcome, Mina," Lisette said as she stepped outside. The sun shone on her smooth brown hair which was pulled back over her ears into a braided bun. Her dark eyes sparkled with life. How pretty she is, Mina thought.

Lisette put her arm around Mina's shoulders, "Come now, and I will show you where you will sleep."

Inside the cabin *Frau* Bickenbach cooked at the hearth. She looked up as they entered, and smiled.

"*Guten Abend*, Mina. Supper will soon be ready." She was a plump, motherly woman, and made Mina feel at home.

Lisette led the way up to the loft. It was dark and hot, and Mina could feel the sweat trickling down her face and neck.

Lisette took a handkerchief out of her pocket and patted her face. "I hope it cools off before bedtime, or we shall never be able to sleep here."

That night a rainstorm came, and the big drops pounded the roof so close above Mina. With the rain came cooler air. The Bickenbachs were already asleep downstairs, but up in the loft a candle still burned. Mina lay on her mattress listening to the rain. Lisette's sister, Frederika, was combing out her long dark hair.

Lisette opened the trunk. "Mina, I think I have a nightgown here that would fit you."

Mina looked down at her own. It was several inches too short for her now. She got up and went over to the trunk.

Lisette held the nightgown up to Mina. It was white cotton with lace and blue ribbon around the neck and hem.

"Oh, *Tante* Lisette, how beautiful."

"You know, Mina, my grandmother in Germany made it for me when I was about your age. So . . . now it is yours." Lisette's eyes glittered in the candlelight.

"Thank you." Mina ran her hands over the smooth white cloth and touched the lace.

Lisette smiled at Mina. "Here, let me undo your

braids." She untied the ribbons and fluffed Mina's hair. Then Lisette uncoiled her own brown shiny hair, and shook it loose. It reached down to her waist, and Mina thought how pretty she looked with her hair flowing down.

"Now, we must go to sleep so that you can be up early for school tomorrow." Lisette blew out the candle.

School again! Mina had almost forgotten. She was anxious to go back to school even if there was no schoolhouse yet. She lay down to sleep, but her eyes did not close. She was thinking of Papa, and wondering where he lay down to sleep that night.

Lisette and Frederika began to breathe the deep breaths of sleep. Mina closed her eyes on the darkness. How dear Lisette was — already like a sister to her, or was she more like a mother?

In the morning, Mina was up early, dressed, washed her face and hands in a pan of water just outside the cabin. She could smell the cornbread cooking over the fire. *Frau* Bickenbach cooked while Lisette and Frederika set the table. Then, together with *Herr* Bickenbach, they ate breakfast.

"Well, Mina, once again you go back to school," said *Herr* Bickenbach, and he bit off a piece of cornbread.

"*Ja*, today I will learn to speak English, I hope."

Everyone laughed.

"Then you must teach me, Mina," Lisette said.

"I will."

As she started on her way to school along Schubert Street, she saw Anna coming from the other direction, and ran to meet her.

"Anna, how is your mother?"

"About the same." Anna looked down at the dirt road. "She still has fever, and is very weak."

A school bell rang sharply through the morning air.

"Let us hurry." Mina took Anna by the hand.

The two girls turned down San Saba Street toward the spreading post oak tree. Lined up underneath its branches were some wooden benches. A few children already sat there, and *Herr* Leyendecker stood facing them, awaiting the rest of his pupils, holding the bell in one hand. He was a strong, robust young man with a broad smile.

As Mina and Anna chose seats on the girls' side, his voice boomed out, "*Guten Morgen*, Mina, *guten Morgen*, Anna."

"*Guten Morgen, Herr* Leyendecker," they replied in chorus.

When all the children had gathered, *Herr* Leyendecker said, "Now we shall begin. First, I want the youngest children on the front row, and the oldest in the back. The rest of you arrange yourselves in between."

After everyone had done as he asked, he continued: "Now, my children, we have yet no books, no paper or pens, and we have only these branches for a roof." He looked upward and spread his arms. "But we have pupils, and we have a teacher. So, we shall begin lessons."

"First, we shall learn to say *guten Morgen* in English. It is — good morn-ing." He exaggerated the formation of each sound with his mouth. "Now, repeat."

"Good morn-ing," all the children answered at once.

Each evening Mina would teach Lisette the English words she had learned that day, and together they practiced pronouncing them.

107

"Your Papa will be so surprised when he returns to hear how much English you have learned, Mina."

After school one day Mina was working in the garden. The hot sun had baked the ground dry and wilted the plants. She had to bring water from the creek, or everything would die. It was hard work, and Mina struggled with the heavy bucket of water up the bank. In spite of her efforts, some of the water sloshed out and onto her feet as she walked, balancing the heavy load with her free arm outstretched. As she set the bucket down on the ground she heard the creaking of a wagon on the road, and then Papa's voice directing the oxen, "Gee, gee," to turn right.

Mina ran toward the road, and there was Papa. He stopped, spread his arms, and she flung herself into them.

At first they said nothing, just held each other tightly. At last Mina released her hold on Papa, and looked at him. His face looked somehow older and tired.

"Papa, what is wrong?" She looked closely into his face for a sign.

"How glad I am to be back with you." Papa smiled his sad smile. Then in answer to her questioning look, he added, "It is nothing, Mina, I am just tired from the journey and the heat." Then he pointed to the back of the wagon. "But look what I have brought you."

There, tied up behind the wagon, was a beautiful spotted milk cow — all reddish brown and white.

"Run, now, get a pail and milk her."

She went to the cow and petted her forehead. As Papa unhitched the oxen Mina filled a pail with foamy white milk. She carried the pail inside, poured some into two cups, and she and Papa drank the warm milk.

108

"Ah," Papa sighed, "it is good to be home. There were so many people sick in New Braunfels, that I am thankful we came to Fredericksburg. The sickness is being brought from Indian Point, I fear."

Papa stood up. "Well, Mina ..." But he did not finish. He put his hand to his forehead, and sat down again.

"What is it, Papa?" Mina felt a pang of alarm.

"Oh, I am just a little dizzy."

"Here, Papa, you must lie down. You are overtired." Mina helped Papa to his bed. When he was lying down, she felt his forehead, and it was burning hot. "Papa, I am afraid you have a fever. I must go for Doctor Schubert."

18

A DREAM

Mina ran all the way to the doctor's cabin. Hurry, hurry was all she could think as she ran.

"Doctor Schubert," Mina called. He appeared in the doorway of the log cabin, wiping his mouth on the back of his hand. "Please come see my Papa. He has a high fever."

The doctor was a large, heavy-set man with a full dark beard.

"Now, now, Mina, do not fret. Your Papa will be all right. He is a strong man."

"But he looks so tired."

Doctor Schubert patted Mina on the head as though she were a little child. "Run along back to your Papa. I will come directly, as soon as my supper is finished."

Mina stood there for a moment. She wanted him to come right now. She did not like being patted on the head.

"No, I will not run along! My Papa is sick, and I

want you to do something about it . . . now." Mina felt fierce. She felt that if Doctor Schubert did not come of his own accord, she would grab him by his beard and drag him there.

She must have looked as fierce as she felt, because Doctor Schubert's mouth fell open. He said nothing for a moment. Then a slow grin broke over his face.

"Well, little *Fräulein*, you have a lot of spirit." Then his face became serious again. "But children do not order grownups about." He pulled on his bushy beard. Mina wondered if he knew she thought of grabbing it. "After supper I will come." With that he turned and went back in the cabin.

Mina felt helpless and alone. She imagined dragging the doctor, kicking and yelling, by his beard down the road. "Children do not order grownups about."

But instead, she turned and ran toward home. It felt good to run. She hated the doctor, she hated having to depend on him for Papa's life.

Outside the cabin she stopped, took a deep breath, and tried to calm herself. She went in to Papa. His eyes were closed, but they fluttered open as she came close to him.

"Doctor Schubert is coming, Papa."

Papa said nothing, but patted Mina's hand on the bed beside him.

After awhile Doctor Schubert did come. Mina waited outside the cabin while he examined Papa. The sky was growing dark, and Mina wished she could hold back the night. At last Doctor Schubert came out.

"Your Papa needs rest, Mina, and you must keep a wet pack on his forehead to cool his fever."

"Very well." Mina looked into the doctor's face

searching for an answer to the question in her mind —
will Papa get well? But she was afraid to ask him.

"I will come back tomorrow to see how he is doing."
And with that Doctor Schubert walked off to the road,
leaving Mina alone to care for Papa during the long
night.

She hurried back into the cabin. The only light was a
candle beside his bed. Papa's eyes were closed. Mina
dampened a cloth, folded it, and placed it gently across
his forehead. She saw that a rash had broken out on his
face and neck.

What can be wrong with Papa? Mina wondered.

That night she sat by Papa's bed without sleeping.
His breathing was shallow and rapid. He groaned and
tossed from side to side, throwing off the wet pack. Mina
hurried to wet it again, and put it back on his forehead.

Suddenly Papa sat bolt upright, his eyes wide open.
"Minchen, Minchen," he exclaimed, and held out his
arms before him.

"Papa!" Mina held him by the shoulders, and tried
to get him to lie down. Papa looked at her, but did not
seem to see her. At last he slumped back on the pillow.
He mumbled some more words, but Mina could not understand.

The candle was burning low now, and there were no
more in the cabin. The flame flickered brightly, and then
went out. Mina could not see Papa's face, but she could
hear his rapid breathing. She thought of the night that
seemed so long ago when Mama had stopped breathing.

"Oh, Papa, do not leave me. Do not leave me all
alone." Saying those words released the sobs Mina had
held back. "Papa ... Papa, do not leave me," she repeated over and over again. Then falling on her knees,
she cried out, "Please, God, help Papa. Do not let him

die." At last she was so exhausted she lay quietly with her head next to Papa's arm. And then she began to dream.

She was riding a horse — fast, so fast that he left the ground. His silky mane flew about Mina's face. It was dark except for the perfectly round moon, and the horse flew straight toward it. As they got closer the moon grew larger and larger until it filled the sky, and Mina was surrounded by white light. In the distance was a dark speck. As they came closer she saw that it was Chief Custaleta. He stood perfectly still, looking at her. His black hair shone in the white light, and Mina's hair in his braid was silvery. He put his hands on the horse's back, swung himself up behind Mina, and away they went. They rode on and on into the moon's light. The light became so bright that Mina had to shield her eyes. Then a glimmering being took shape. It was an ancient Indian with white hair.

"Can you help my Papa?" Mina asked.

The Indian nodded his head.

There was a moaning sound, and Mina awoke. It was morning. She lifted her head from Papa's bed, and heard him moan again. He was still burning with fever, but now Mina knew what she must do. Dreams were not to be ignored. God spoke to Joseph in Egypt through dreams. And now He had spoken to Mina.

19

LISETTE AND THE SHAMAN

Mina remembered how an Indian had cured a man on the way to Fredericksburg. Maybe Indian medicine could help Papa too. It was a hope at least.

But Mina did not dare to leave Papa alone in the cabin. She thought of Lisette. *Ja*, she must run and fetch Lisette to stay with Papa while she went to the Indian camp.

She wet the pack again and placed it on Papa's forehead. He stirred. Mina kissed him lightly on the cheek, and went outside. The sky was just beginning to lighten, and the air was cool and fresh.

Mina ran all the way to the Bickenbachs' cabin. The door was open, and someone was stirring about inside. *Frau* Bickenbach appeared.

"Why Mina, what brings you here at dawn?"

"My Papa is sick, and I came to ask *Tante* Lisette if she would help me."

"Oh, I am sorry to hear that . . . but I know Lisette will come." *Frau* Bickenbach pointed up to the loft. "You just go on up."

When Mina got up to the dark loft, she could see Lisette's form sitting up in bed. Mina did not want to awaken Frederika, so she whispered.

"*Tante* Lisette, Papa is very sick, and I need your help." Mina paused while she mustered the courage to tell Lisette her plan.

"Oh my," Lisette touched Mina's arm. "Of course, Mina, how can I help?"

"Will you stay with Papa while I go for the Indian medicine man?"

Lisette gasped. "Mina, you cannot!"

"I must."

"But, Mina, Doctor Schubert . . ."

"He did not help Papa," Mina interrupted. "*Tante* Lisette, listen, I had a dream last night. I dreamed that I went to an old Indian who said he could cure Papa."

Lisette looked at Mina for a moment in silence. "Then it must be God's will." She began to dress quickly. "You run back to your Papa. I will come." As Mina started to leave, Lisette added, "Do not say anything about it to my mother."

Mina nodded silently.

When she got back to the cabin Papa was still asleep. She poured a cup of water and put it on the box beside Papa's bed. Then she got the blue beaded belt and fastened it around her waist. It was up to her, Mina thought. What happened to Papa was up to her. She took a deep breath, straightened her shoulders, and went outside to wait.

At last Lisette came.

"Are you sure about this, Mina?"

"*Ja.*"

115

"But Indians . . . you cannot tell what they might do."

"Chief Custaleta is my friend. He would not let anyone harm me."

"I do not think your Papa would like it, Mina."

"But I cannot let Papa die the way Mama did." Mina's throat tightened. "I have to do something. And God has told me what to do!" Tears began to stream down Mina's cheeks.

Lisette took Mina in her arms. "I understand, Mina." After a moment Lisette loosened her arms and held Mina out from her looking into her face intently. "Be very careful."

Mina wiped the tears away. "*Ja*, I will." Then she turned and headed for the Indian camp down by the river. She broke into a run, for she was anxious to get help for Papa. She slowed to a walk to catch her breath, and then ran again.

At the river Mina walked along the bank until she came opposite the camp. Indian women were dipping their water baskets in the river and carrying them back up to camp. Mina watched from behind some bushes. Then a young girl came down to the river's edge, and Mina saw that it was Amaya.

Drawing a deep breath Mina stepped out from behind the bush and waved at Amaya. The girl looked startled at first. But then she smiled, put down the water basket, and ran back toward camp. The women stood watching Mina.

In a few moments Amaya reappeared astride a horse and rode across the river to where Mina stood. She dismounted, and the two girls looked at one another. Mina did not know how to tell her about Papa.

Without thinking Mina said, "My Papa is sick."

Amaya cocked her head and looked at Mina, not understanding.

Mina thought for a moment. How can I make her understand? Then Mina pointed to herself with both hands and repeated, "My." She reached up high with one hand, "Papa." Here she rubbed her cheeks with both hands to describe a beard.

Amaya was watching her closely and said a word that sounded something like "Papa?" with a question in her voice.

"*Ja*, that is right!" Then Mina lay down upon the ground and groaned. "Is sick," Mina finished her sentence, and looked at Amaya.

The Indian girl seemed to understand. She led the horse to a large boulder, and holding him by the mane, helped Mina get on. Then Amaya pulled herself on in front.

The horse stepped carefully through the river, lifting his hoofs high. Once in the camp Amaya stopped the horse and dismounted. She said a word to Mina and went into a tipi. Mina slid off the horse but remained close beside him. The horse whinnied and shook his mane, stomping one hoof.

Indians began to gather. Men emerged from their tipis, and women came up from the river and gathered around. Everyone looked at Mina. One squaw pointed at Mina's blue beaded belt, and said something to another. The Indians drew closer and closer. Mina wanted to bolt and run, but she could not move. Her heart began to thump within her chest. It was different when a few of these Indians came to Fredericksburg to trade, but now Mina was alone in the middle of their camp — surrounded.

To Mina's relief Amaya came back with her father,

and spoke to him, pointing at Mina. Chief Custaleta looked at Mina, but he did not smile. He uttered some words. Mina heard one that she had learned — "Shaman" — and she knew that it meant medicine man.

They do understand, Mina thought, and he is going to help. Then she thought of Papa lying on the bed, flushed with fever.

"Please hurry," Mina pleaded.

Even though the Indians did not know the words, they seemed to understand the urgency in her voice. Soon the Shaman appeared.

Mina had never seen such an old man with so few clothes on — only a loin cloth. His dark leathery skin sagged on his thin frame. His long white hair was thick and coarse, like the man in her dream. He had not a tooth in his head, and seemed to be chewing on his cud as he eyed Mina silently. In his hand he held a drawstring pouch.

The Shaman's horse was brought, and a young warrior helped him up. He sat astride his horse, still chewing his cud. He tied the pouch to the wooden saddle frame, and made a sound, "Unnh."

Chief Custaleta mounted his horse, and reached out his hand to Mina. He pulled her up on his horse behind him, and they started down the bank, splashed through the river, and up the other side toward Fredericksburg.

20

INDIAN MEDICINE

They moved slowly and silently through the woods, and did not go by the road. The chief and Mina were in the lead, and the old Shaman followed behind. Custaleta smelled slightly rancid, and his bare back glistened with oil. His long hair was doubled up and held by silver hair tubes. Mina looked back at the old Shaman. His eyes were closed.

As they neared Fredericksburg, Chief Custaleta reined in his horse, turned and looked down at Mina. In his proud eyes there was a question, and he spoke a single word. Mina understood and pointed the direction to their cabin — just across the creek from where they had stopped. Smoke was rising from the chimney. Lisette must have made a fire, Mina thought.

Custaleta dismounted and motioned for Mina to climb down. Then the chief tied his horse to a tree, and went to hold the old man's horse.

The Shaman dismounted. As he turned to his horse

to unfasten the pouch, the sun shone on his long white hair, and it seemed to glow like the sun itself. He fastened the little bag at his waist, nodded to Custaleta, and they began to make their way toward Mina's cabin on foot. They moved quietly, and Mina followed behind.

Once across the creek and onto their lot, Mina ran ahead to the cabin. She looked inside.

"Mina!" Lisette stood up as Mina appeared. Her eyes looked startled.

"It is all right, *Tante* Lisette. Chief Custaleta and the Shaman have come. How is Papa?"

"Just the same," Lisette answered.

Mina looked back out the door. The two Indians stood almost hidden in the trees.

Mina returned to them. "Come," she said to Custaleta, and made a motion for him to follow her to the cabin.

Custaleta took the Shaman by one arm and helped him along. At the door they hesitated for a moment and then entered. Lisette caught her breath and put her hand over her mouth as if to stifle a scream.

Mina thought the Indians looked strangely out of place and a little uncomfortable inside the cabin. Custaleta remained to one side of the door. But the Shaman got right to work.

He squatted on the earthen floor near Papa and unrolled a hide, spreading it before him. Now he opened the little pouch he had brought along and began to remove its contents and placed them carefully on the hide. First he pulled out a small doll—about three inches tall — made of a stuffed animal skin. It was painted bright colors and had long black hair. The Shaman held the doll by a thin leather loop attached to its head. He dangled it before his face, and said some sing-song

words. As he sang to the doll he jerked it about so that the doll appeared to dance.

Papa lay still, and only the movement of his chest up and down showed that he was alive. Mina looked at Lisette. She had not moved since the Indians came in, but was frozen beside the fireplace, watching the Shaman.

Then the old Indian pulled out a small skin bag. He turned to Mina. *"Agua caliente."*

Mina did not understand. "What?"

"Agua caliente," the Shaman repeated, pointed to the fire and then to the small bag.

Mina looked at Lisette.

"It is Spanish, I think," Lisette said.

The Shaman emptied the contents of the bag into his hand and showed it to Mina. It looked like ground up leaves of some kind.

Then Mina understood. "Oh, he wants hot water." She ran to the fireplace where a teakettle of water was already heating, picked up Papa's cup, and came back to the Shaman.

As Mina knelt on the earthen floor and held the cup out toward him, the Shaman poured some of the ground leaves into the cup, nodding his head. This done he motioned Mina toward the fireplace. Mina filled the cup

121

with steaming water, brought it back to the Shaman, and placed it on the hide beside the doll.

The Shaman nodded once to Mina, and reached again into his bag. This time he pulled out a piece of wood on which hung hollow cylinders made of bone. With a smooth stick he struck each one, and began to chant.

Hai ya, ho la,
Hai ya, ho la.

He repeated this over and over.

Papa stirred. He opened his eyes, raised himself up on his elbows, and looked about the room incredulously. "Mina, what ...?" But he fell weakly back onto his pillow.

Mina rushed to his side and knelt by the bed. "It is all right, Papa." She smoothed his rumpled hair back from his forehead. "The Indian medicine man is here. He has many cures for sickness, Papa. He will cure you."

"Oh, Mina, no," Papa groaned.

"*Ja*, Papa, he will cure you."

The Shaman grunted to Mina and held out the cup of tea. Mina took it.

"Here, Papa, you must drink this."

Lisette helped hold Papa up enough so he could sip a little tea. It steamed up before his face. Then he took another sip, and another until the cup was empty.

"Very good, Papa." Mina turned to look at the Shaman. He was nodding his head in approval. Then he put everything back in the bag, rolled up the hide, and rose slowly on his thin bowed legs. He handed Mina the bag of tea leaves. Custaleta came and took the old man's arm. They started for the door, slowly.

Mina wanted to give the Shaman something for

122

helping Papa. She thought of the little hand mirror Auntie Fischer had given her, and got it from the trunk by the fireplace. She pointed to herself with her thumb and then to the Shaman with her forefinger the way she had seen Indians at the market make signs.

The Shaman stopped, turned to look at Mina. He reached out his hand and took the mirror, nodding his head solemnly. Then they left as they had come — without a sound.

Mina went to the door and watched them until they were out of sight. Then she looked back at Papa. He was watching her, and he smiled weakly. He opened his mouth to speak.

"Mina . . ."

"Do not talk yet, Papa." Mina put a wet pack on Papa's forehead. "Just rest now."

Papa closed his eyes and seemed to sink into the bed with a sigh.

Lisette motioned to Mina to come outside with her. It was midday, and the sun was hot.

"Mina," Lisette put her hand under Mina's chin, "as your Papa always says, you are a real pioneer girl."

Suddenly Mina went weak all over. She did not feel like a pioneer girl. Instead she longed to be comforted like a child. She remembered once when she was a very little girl in Wehrstedt, she had fallen down and bumped her head. Mama held her, rocking back and forth in the creaky rocker.

Mina looked at Lisette. "I am so tired."

Lisette put her arms around Mina. "Everything is going to be all right." She patted Mina softly on the back as she held her close. "I will return this evening and bring some broth for Papa. It will give him strength. And I will sit up with him tonight so you may sleep."

"Oh, thank you, *Tante* Lisette." Mina waved as Lisette went off down the road.

She did come that evening, and every day. Papa's fever left. One day as Lisette was feeding Papa, Mina watched his face. She saw him looking at Lisette with his big sad eyes. Lisette looked down, a smile on her face.

That night before going to bed Mina sat beside Papa. She did not know how to begin to tell Papa how she felt about Lisette, how she seemed to belong in their family . . . how Mina wished Papa would marry her! She knew Papa was fond of Lisette, and she knew Lisette cared for Papa.

"Papa, do you care for *Tante* Lisette?" Mina blurted out suddenly.

Papa looked startled at the question. Then he smiled and put his hand over Mina's. "Well, Mina, she has been very kind to me, to us, while I have been sick."

"She is very pretty, is she not, Papa?"

Papa chuckled. "*Jawohl.*"

"Then why not ask her to marry you, Papa? You know Mama would not want you to be lonely, and she would want me to have a mother." The words came tumbling out. "I know she would say yes, Papa, I just know it."

Then Papa became serious. "Give me a little time to think, Mina." He patted her hand. "Time to go to bed now."

Papa grew strong again, strong enough to work in the garden. And Mina knew that before long he would be making trips in the wagon to earn some more money.

One evening after the heat of the day was over, Mina and Papa were working in their garden.

"*Guten Abend,*" came a familiar voice from the road.

It was Lisette. She was carrying a bundle under her arm.

Papa straightened up from his hoeing. Mina ran to meet her.

"I have something for you, Mina." Lisette unrolled the bundle. It was a dress made of yellow calico with a wide ruffle around the bottom.

"Oh, *Tante* Lisette," Mina threw her arms around her, "Thank you, thank you."

"Go, try it on," Lisette urged.

Mina hurried into the cabin, pulled off her dress and put the new one over her head. It had many tiny buttons down the back. Mina swirled once to make the ruffle flare out, then ran out to Lisette and Papa.

"Here, Mina, let me button you," Lisette moved toward Mina.

As she worked with the buttons, Papa suddenly blurted out, "Lisette, I think it is time we get married."

Lisette left off buttoning Mina, and they both turned to look at Papa. For a moment no one said anything, and Papa's words hung in the air between them.

Mina looked at Lisette. Her dark eyes were sparkling with life. Then Mina ran to Papa, took his hand, and pulled him along to Lisette. Taking Lisette by the hand, Mina pleaded, "Say yes, *Tante* Lisette, please say yes."

"Oh, yes," Lisette said with such enthusiasm that the three began to dance around in a circle.

Mina looked at Papa. His face glowed with health and happiness. She did not know whether the Shaman had cured Papa or whether Lisette's love had done it. All she knew was that Papa was well, and that their family would be whole again.

125

GLOSSARY OF GERMAN WORDS

auf Wiedersehen	farewell, goodbye
Frau	Mrs.
Fräulein	Miss, young lady
fröhliche Weihnachten	Merry Christmas
guten Abend	good evening
guten Morgen	good morning
guten Tag	good day
Herr	Mr.
ja (ya)	yes
jawohl (yavohl)	yes indeed
kleine (klinah)	little
lebe wohl	farewell, goodbye
Leiterwagen	farm wagon
nein	no
Opa (short for *Grosspapa*)	grandpa
Tannenbaum	fir tree, Christmas tree
Tante	aunt

CPSIA information can be obtained at www.ICGtesting.com
Printed in the USA
BVOW071456140713

325880BV00002B/19/P

9 780890 155066